REAL SOLUTIONS
for Overcoming Discouragement, Rejection, and the Blues

D1113553

REAL SOLUTIONS
for Overcoming Discouragement, Rejection, and the Blues

H. Norman Wright

SERVANT PUBLICATIONS
ANN ARBOR, MICHIGAN

Vine Books is an imprint of Servant Publications especially designed to
serve evangelical Christians.

Published by Servant Publications
P.O. Box 8617
Ann Arbor, Michigan 48107

Cover design by Uttley/DouPonce DesignWorks—Sisters, Oregon

01 02 03 04 10 9 8 7 6 5 4 3 2 1

Printed in the United States of America
ISBN 1-56955-240-1

Library of Congress Cataloging-in-Publication Data

Wright, H. Norman.
    Real solutions for overcoming discouragement, rejection, and the
blues / H. Norman Wright.
        p. cm.
    Includes bibliographical references.
    ISBN 1-56955-240-1 (alk. paper)
        1. Depression, Mental—Religious aspects—Christianity. I. Title.

BV4910.34 .W75 2001
248.8'625—dc21

                                                                2001026034

Contents

Chapter 1

Fighting Discouragement: Going for Broke

It doesn't feel good. It takes the edge off life and drains you of your motivation. It puts a damper on every other area of your life. What am I talking about? Discouragement. It can take the heart right out of you. It's not a fun experience but, rather, a state of misery. You can end up aching all over.

Have you been there? If you're human, you have been. It's part of life, though we might wish otherwise. Perhaps you, like many others, have made the statement: "I'm *so* discouraged." People describe discouragement in various ways.

- "It took the wind right out of my sails."
- "It felt like I was knocked right off my feet."
- "It sucked my drive and energy right out of me."
- "It was a form of paralysis. Physically I could move but in another sense I couldn't."
- "The daylight looked dark even though the sun was out."

So what is this malady called discouragement? Look at the word and take it apart. You find the word *courage*, with its root syllable *cor.* This is the Latin word for *heart*, which is the center of this condition. Discouragement is literally the loss of heart. When discouragement enters into our lives, hope exits. When discouragement gains a foothold, we are tempted to give up. The psalmist felt this way: "Come, Lord, and show me your mercy, for I am helpless, overwhelmed, in deep distress; my problems go from bad to worse. Oh, save me from them all!" (Ps 25:16-17, LB).

Many people we read about in the Scriptures were tempted to give up at one time or another, yet the Bible is a book of hope. Addressing all of us, Paul says, "For everything that was written in the past was written to teach us, so that through endurance and the encouragement of the Scriptures we might have hope" (Rom 15:4).

There are reasons why we become discouraged.

Have you ever worked at something for a long time and yet not seen any change? I've heard it so often:

- "For the past twenty years I've poured myself into this marriage and nothing seems to do any good."
- "I'm getting weary because of where I am financially. I've worked really hard, even held two jobs, but we never seem to get out of the hole. It's not worth all this exhaustion."
- "I'm getting so discouraged about men. Everyone I date seems to be weird or noncommittal. Aren't there any possibilities out there?"

A friend of mine interviewed three times a week for six months, looking for a job. Some places said, "We'll call," or, "It looks hopeful," or, "You could be just the one we're looking for," but nothing happened. Discouragement—it settles in like a dense fog to block out the light of hope.

Have you ever worked hard at something and felt, "Yes, things will be different; we're getting somewhere," only to find that you haven't gotten anywhere? You put in extra time at work, and your evaluations get high marks. You can just taste that promotion, but it goes to someone else. It wasn't that person's ability; he or she "knew someone" who pulled strings, or so it seems.

What about all the time, energy, sacrifice, and money you put into raising a child? You model Christian values, go to church, send him to camp and church schools, and one day he steals a car.

In some seasons of life, you may experience an overload of problems all at one time. It's not that one of them by itself couldn't be handled, but put them all together and you feel "it's too much," and "too much" may put you into a state of crisis! It's like the western singer lamenting that he lost his job, his girlfriend left him, his dog died, and now his truck won't run.

I've heard people say discouragement is not a good place to be in. That's true. So how can we make use of it for our benefit? Could its presence cause us to reconsider what we're doing and come up with a different or better approach? Could its presence cause us to realize that our own resources are insufficient and we need to rely more upon God and his wisdom?[1] It's something to consider.

Unrealistic Expectations

One cause of discouragement for many is unrealistic expectations. Some have expectations for themselves, for others, for their marriages that can be met only in the unreality of their minds. Perfectionists, often those with the highest expectations, can live in a constant state of discouragement; I've never yet met a successful perfectionist.

Most of us would like to be successful. Some of us, however, turn success into a requirement. When this happens, we become preoccupied with the pursuit of perfection.

To prove that they are good enough, perfectionists strive to do the impossible. They set lofty goals and see no reason why they should not achieve them. But soon perfectionists are overwhelmed by the arduous tasks they've set for themselves. If you're a perfectionist, your standards are so high no one could constantly attain them. They're beyond reach and beyond reason. The strain of reaching is continual, but the goals are impossible. And the result is discouragement.

Perfectionism is a thief. It offers rewards but it actually steals joy and satisfaction.

When you require perfection of yourself, you assign your life to a set of rules. These often come in the form of "I must," "I should," and "I ought to."

Perfectionists have a need for certainty, not risk. They're comfortable about only those activities in which they are sure of the outcomes. When the certainty is lacking, they can actually make themselves sick by worrying over the right decision. Afraid of failure, they will not attempt to accomplish anything unless they are sure of success.

The fear of not being perfect can cause delays and excuses and turn a perfectionist into a procrastinator. The fear of not being perfect immobilizes.

As long as we cling to the ideal of perfection, we will never be good enough in our own eyes. Inside each of us is a critical voice that is able to shred our best efforts. No matter how well we do, we could have done more. This inner critic draws our attention to each limitation, each flaw. Its voice is shrill and demanding, a composite of all the outer judges we have known in our lives: "You never do anything right. Look what a mess you made of things." "You ought to know better. How could you make such a stupid remark?"

Perfectionism thrives on comparisons. Yet nothing gets us down faster than measuring our achievements against those of others. In the process we almost always idealize others while minimizing our own gifts: "Look at how clean she keeps her house. And her kids are all doing so well. I'm so inadequate. What's the matter with me that I can't hold it all together?" All in all, we find that we are never as good, smart, or efficient as others. Working harder does not help, as some defect always remains.[2]

Whenever we're discouraged we need to ask ourselves if we're being perfectionists. Perfectionism is not a spiritual gift or calling. It's a chosen journey to "being sufficient," but the payoff is discouragement. Remember that God has already declared us to be sufficient through what he has done for us through Jesus Christ.

Unwelcome Adversity

Well, what about discouragement caused by adversity, that unwelcome companion in life? It's a major cause for discouragement. What can we do?

Paul learned how to deal with adversity. "We are hard pressed on every side, but not crushed; perplexed, but not in despair; persecuted, but not abandoned; struck down, but not destroyed" (1 Cor 4:8-9).

Paul also said, "Therefore we do not lose heart. Though

outwardly we are wasting away, yet inwardly we are being renewed day by day. For our light and momentary troubles are achieving for us an eternal glory that far outweighs them all" (2 Cor 4:16-17).

Fresh strength is what every discouraged person needs. Where are you getting your strength?

God is the Source of this strength. The phrase to remember in the midst of discouragement is God's words to Joshua, "Be strong and courageous." God continues, "Do not be terrified; do not be discouraged, for the Lord your God will be with you wherever you go" (Jos 1:9). God *is* the Source of our strength.

Scripture gives us other resources as well.

For while we are in this tent, we groan and are burdened, because we do not wish to be unclothed but to be clothed with our heavenly dwelling, so that what is mortal may be swallowed up by life. Now it is God who has made us for this very purpose and has given us the Spirit as a deposit, guaranteeing what is to come. Therefore we are always confident.

2 CORINTHIANS 5:4-6

We come to the place where we're able to say, "This makes us confident. *No matter what happens.*" This is an attitude, a personal choice. Do you know what the word *attitude* means? Attitude is a manner of acting, thinking, or feeling that shows one's disposition, opinion, or mental set.

Chuck Swindoll described it this way:

The longer I live, the more I realize the impact of attitude on my life. Attitude, to me, is more important than facts. It is more important than the past, than education, than money, than circumstances, than failures, than successes, than what other people think or say or do. It is more important than appearance, giftedness, or skill. It will make or break a company ... a church ... a home. The remarkable thing is we have a choice every day regarding the attitude we will embrace for that day. We cannot change our past; we cannot change the fact that people will act in a certain way; we cannot change the inevitable. The only thing we can do is play on the one string we have, and that is our attitude.... I am convinced that life is 10% what happens to me and 90% how I react to it.[3]

This attitude of confidence has worked for many who faced and lived with physical adversity. It worked for John Milton who was blind. He wrote *Paradise Lost* and *Paradise Regained.* It also worked for Beethoven, who, in spite of his deafness, gave us the Ninth Symphony. It worked for John Bunyan, who wrote *Pilgrim's Progress* while in prison. And remember Helen Keller, who was deaf and blind? She said, "Neither darkness nor silence can impede the progress of the human spirit."[4]

Is it possible to regain courage even when you are discouraged? Yes. Scripture contains many messages about fighting discouragement:

This is the message of Job, who had lost virtually everything but his life: "Though he slay me, yet will I hope in him; I will surely defend my ways to his face" (Job 13:15).

This is the message of David: "Even though I walk through the valley of the shadow of death, I will fear no evil, for you are with me; your rod and your staff, they comfort me" (Ps 23:4).

This is the message of Isaiah: "You will keep in perfect

peace him whose mind is steadfast, because he trusts in you" (Is 26:3).

This is the message of Paul: "For I am convinced that neither death nor life, neither angels nor demons, neither the present nor the future, nor any powers, neither height nor depth, nor anything else in all creation, will be able to separate us from the love of God that is in Christ Jesus our Lord" (Rom 8:38-39).

In his book *Courage for Crisis Living*, Paul Walker tells of a family overcoming the crisis of discouragement:

> I met a man in Austin, Texas, and while waiting for a banquet to start, asked him how things were going. In answer, he said, "You might say that my family is on the comeback trail." "The comeback trail? That sounds interesting. What does it mean?" I asked. In answer, he related that just two years prior he had been a very wealthy man. The recession hit. He wasn't ready. He lost everything he had. He turned to alcohol. His wife turned to activities outside the home. His eldest son turned to drugs, and in his words, "My whole family was tearing apart." (That would be enough to discourage anyone).
>
> "Then," he said, "one day my wife came to me and said she couldn't stand it any longer. She wanted a divorce." This was the last straw. He called a family conference and said, "We've got to do something about this. We can't go on like this anymore. What are we going to do?" To his surprise his twelve-year-old daughter stood up and said, "Daddy, the first thing we have to remember is that God still loves us."
>
> Like a thunderbolt out of the sky, it hit them. "God

still loves us." The family took inventory. They had lost everything tangible, but so what? It was wood, brick, chrome, and a little bit of this and a little bit of that.

Then he said, "We still had each other. We still had our health. We had opportunity, and we still had God." "So," he said, "we got on our knees and prayed for God's guidance. From that moment on we started on the comeback trail. I swallowed my pride and took a menial job. My wife went to work. The children are helping, and we have become a close-knit unit because we have really learned that God still loves us."

This is the way to handle distress: "God still loves us."[5]

Even if you don't feel it, can you say it? "God still loves me." What would happen to your discouragement if you said this each hour of the day?

Taking a Risk

Yes, it takes a risk to confront discouragement and say, "You're out of here. I don't want you controlling my life anymore."

Perhaps one of the best ways to identify the steps involved in taking any risk is by considering the example of passing another car on a two-lane highway. Once or twice a year I travel a twenty-five-mile stretch of highway in the high desert area of Southern California. It isn't my favorite stretch of road because of the limitation of the two lanes and the frequent dips in the road that tend to hide oncoming cars.

When I'm stuck behind a slow driver, I have the choice of staying behind him or looking for an opportunity to pass.

When I think about passing, I must not only observe the slow vehicle I'm following, but also watch for oncoming traffic. Then I have to determine if there is enough highway between me and the approaching cars to allow me to pass.

These are the stages in taking the risk of passing on the highway: preparing and assessing adequately, making a commitment, then following through by pressing the accelerator to the floor, surging around the slow driver, and moving back into the right lane. This process is successful for most people when they follow all the procedures. However, it doesn't work for the driver who hesitates and vacillates when pulling out into the oncoming lane. Losing nerve and not accelerating properly can lead to a tragic accident.

Similarly, when we risk and choose to do something about our discouragement, we must be committed to follow through if we are to get out of the slow lane and get "unstuck."

I would rather choose to take a risk than be forced into taking one. Which would you prefer? If we postpone taking risks when they are needed, we may be forced to accept something we don't want or to take risks when we are least prepared for them.

Howard Hughes, one of the richest men of the twentieth century, is a good example of what can happen to someone who refuses to take risks. As a young man Hughes greatly impacted the aircraft industry with bold risks for change, helping the United States maintain dominance in the sky during wartime. He helped establish the movie industry and influenced the entertainment industry. He gained tremendous power that affected world history.

Howard Hughes was a pioneer risk taker for much of his life. But then he changed his attitude, becoming a fanatic at protecting himself against risk. He created a virtual prison for himself, insulating himself from decisions, people, germs, or anything else he perceived to be a threat. Hughes was worth billions, but he chose to vegetate in a hotel room until he died. He ended up a fearful old man who didn't trust anyone, a prisoner when he could have been free.[6]

When Howard Hughes stopped risking, discouragement and despair got the best of him.

If we don't risk, our world grows smaller. It shrinks. We become comfortable with sameness and stagnation. We invest our energy in keeping life the way it is. We resist growth. We become reactors rather than making things happen. When we don't risk, we are the losers. We stay in the holes of our discouragement. When we don't risk stepping out, we risk missing the life-abundant changes God has in store for us.[7]

When you're disappointed, there's an experience that continues to live in your life. It could have happened last week or six months ago, but still it lives on, controlling your future. Many people have their futures dictated by their pasts. It doesn't have to be that way. We have more of a choice with disappointment than we do with depression.

It's easy to allow events or incidents to make us bitter. And it's understandable. If anyone could have become bitter, it was Paul.

They say they serve Christ? I know I sound like a madman, but I have served him far more! I have worked harder, been put in jail more often, been whipped times without number and faced death again and again. Five different times the Jews gave me thirty-nine lashes. Three times I was beaten with rods. Once I was stoned. Three times I was shipwrecked. Once I spent a whole night and a day adrift at sea. I have traveled many weary miles. I have faced danger from flooded rivers and from robbers. I have faced danger from my own people, the Jews, as well as from the Gentiles. I have faced danger in the cities, in the deserts, and on the stormy seas. And I have faced danger from men who claim to be Christians but are not. I have lived with weariness and pain and sleepless nights. Often I have been hungry and thirsty and have gone without food. Often I have shivered with cold, without enough clothing to keep me warm.

2 CORINTHIANS 11:23-27, NLT

Our hurts from the past are like abscesses—raw, oozing wounds that become covered by scabs. But from time to time the scabs peel off. Unfortunately, what is uncovered is not the complete growth of restored life, but the same raw sore.

Many people travel through life with such unhealed emotional wounds. They carry them in their memories. The capacity for being affected by the past actually increases as we age; the older we get, the more we have to remember, and our lives, to some degree, are reflections of our memories. Our present feelings, such as joy, sorrow, anger, grief, and contentment, are more dependent upon the way we remember events than upon the events themselves. The greater the length of time between an event and the present, the greater the potential for distortion. Who we are today is a product of how we remember our past events.[8]

We're not meant to become stuck in the events of the past. "Therefore, if anyone is in Christ, he is a new creation; the old has gone, the new has come!" (2 Cor 5:17).

It was possible for Paul to let the past go and not direct his present life. It's all right to reach out and risk again. Discouragement tends to diminish our risk-taking ability for we don't want to be hurt again. I see it in the woman who was disappointed in a love relationship. The boy who didn't make the team the first time around. The budding author whose first manuscript was rejected. Too often we push the same buttons we've been pushing for years, and our past comes flashing up on the screen again.

Why try? It will only be a repeat. Sometimes we inadvertently and unintentionally bring about the past by what we think and do. It makes a difference as you look at the present and the future if you see it through Philippians 4:8: "Finally, brothers, whatever is true, whatever is noble, whatever is right, whatever is pure, whatever is lovely, whatever is admirable—if anything is excellent or praiseworthy—think about such things."

For the future to be different, we need to reach.

For the future to be different, we need to hope.

When we're discouraged, we don't have hope. But hope is an antidote to discouragement.

We use the word *hope* so glibly. It's also easy to misuse it. Have you ever said, "I hope it comes in the mail today," or, "I hope I get that raise," or, "I hope they are able to visit this year"? Every time we use the word *hope* in that way we are expressing a desire, but we are also wishing for something that is uncertain. In a way we are saying, "I don't know for certain if this is going to happen. It might or might not, but I wish it would."

That's not the biblical definition of hope. In the Scriptures, hope is solid, sure. It is a certainty. There are no "maybe's" or "I hope so's" about it. In the Bible, "hope is man's eager expectation of something that God has promised will certainly happen in the future."[9]

There's no question but that God's promises will be kept. They are certain.

Hope is not blind optimism; it's realistic optimism. People of hope are always aware of the struggles and difficulties of life, but they live beyond those struggles with a sense of potential and possibility. They are not impossibility thinkers.

People of hope don't live only for the possibilities of tomorrow, but they see the possibilities of today, even when it's not going well.

People of hope don't just long for what they're missing in life, but they experience what they have already received.

People of hope can say an emphatic *no* to stagnation and an energetic *yes* to life. Hope is allowing God's Spirit to set us free and draw us forward in our lives.[10]

For the future to be different, we need to do something.

Paul said, "I press on toward the goal ..." (Phil 3:14). But what does it mean "to press"? Actually it is a very important phrase that we use in many different ways. "To press" is to push as you push a button. "To press" is to exert pressure such as pressing or ironing clothes. "To press" is to make a great exertion as the weightlifter does when he "snatches" and "presses" several hundred pounds above his head. "To press" is to gamble, and it means go for broke. "To press" is to relentlessly pursue or intensely go after.[11]

Why not go for broke? Press on. It's much better to be in the process of doing something than to be overwhelmed by discouragement. Go back and reread the Scriptures mentioned earlier. Read them every day. Let them be your source of encouragement as you walk away from discouragement.

Chapter 2

Rejection—It Hurts

Do you remember hearing statements such as these? Have any been directed at you over the years?

- "I don't want you on my team."
- "I don't like you."
- "I don't love you."
- "Don't bother me. Can't you see I'm busy!"
- "I'm sorry, but we can't use your services."
- "You just won't work out in our organization."
- "Go to your room. We don't want you at the same table."
- "Sorry, but we will not accept your article."
- "You have to change. You're just not good enough the way you are."
- "I'm disappointed in you."
- "You couldn't have made that. It looks too good."

Simple statements, short statements. But they all can cause a great deal of pain. Statements like these hurt us no matter how much we say, "It doesn't matter." Being rejected hurts.

You can feel rejection whether you are single or married. And perhaps rejection from a marriage partner is one of life's ultimate hurts. The closer you are to someone, the more it hurts when that person shows disapproval or says, "I don't want you anymore."

We're all afraid of rejection. And each time it occurs, our fear intensifies. The fear of rejection tempts us to deny who we really are in order to succeed in getting acceptance and love. But if we experience enough rejection, discouragement or in some cases depression sets in.

Have you ever been rejected by ...

- A look?
- A shrug?
- Silence?
- A raised eyebrow?
- A sneer?
- A back turned on you?
- The word *no?*
- Not being chosen for a team or a project?
- A tone of voice?

When you experience any of these, how do you feel? For most it's the feeling of being left out.

Poor Alice felt rejected at the Mad Hatter's tea party in *Alice in Wonderland* by Lewis Carroll.

> The table was a large one, but the three were all crowded together at one corner of it: "No room! No room!" they cried out when they saw Alice coming.
>
> "There's *plenty* of room," said Alice indignantly, and she sat down in a large armchair at one end of the table.
>
> "Have some wine," the March Hare said in an encouraging tone.
>
> Alice looked all around the table, but there was nothing on it but tea. "I don't see any wine," she remarked.
>
> "There isn't any," said the March Hare....
>
> "Your hair wants cutting," said the Hatter....
>
> "You should learn not to make personal remarks," Alice said with some severity: "it's very rude."[1]

People make "personal remarks"—intentionally or unintentionally—and we feel rejection.

Every rejection we experience is like throwing cold water on our hopes and dreams.

What part does the past or present rejection play in our lives? We equate being different with rejection.

One woman said:

We are all at times "different" and thus become vulnerable to rejection. As a child I was very prone to strep throat and severe joint pains which made the threat of rheumatic fever always present. At some point in my early teens I was ordered by my doctor to stay at home from school for a semester. Instantly I became different. I used to watch through the window as other kids went to school and came home again. Teachers wrote me notes saying, "Don't worry, your health is most important," but I hardly related to what they were saying. All I knew were the long, lonely hours I spent at home and the many trips I made to the doctor. And above all, my friends for the most part went their own way because I wasn't any fun. I couldn't do things. Now I wasn't a worse person because I lacked physical stamina, but I felt rejectable nevertheless.[2]

Feeling Rejectable

Some of us end up being especially sensitive to any hint of rejection. And because of this tendency, we see rejection in statements and actions when it's not even there. We live with the residue of previous rejections. Every rejection we've experienced in the past causes us to be overly sensitive to a recurrence in the present. The pain of previous experiences stays with us; it haunts us.

Elizabeth Skoglund describes what happens:

> Whether ... rejection is warranted or not, great or small, rejection is a painful experience which it is not desirable to repeat. Yet how often all of us recollect our past injustices and rejections until their memories can indeed be more vivid now than they were at the time.
>
> The problem with a feeling such as rejection is that it stays, persists, eats away at us until it has the capacity to erode and destroy our lives.[3]

Judy was a young woman who actually looked as if she was afraid of rejection. When she came into the room, her eyes pleaded, "Accept me; tell me I'm all right." She was starving for approval and overly sensitive to any look or remark that even hinted of nonacceptance. She was certain that others did not want her around. She read rejection into neutral or even positive conversation. And she was good at it since she *expected* to be rejected. Unfortunately, even when others were friendly and accepting, she was suspicious of them. In her words, "If I trust them, who's to say it's not some trick on their part? They'll just reject me when I'm not looking, and because I trusted them, it will hurt even worse!" Judy's fear of rejection was consuming her. So when it came to building any kind of a relationship, she was discouraged because she felt it was doomed to fail.

Childhood Patterns

Some who are afraid of rejection come from homes where they were treated as unacceptable or unwanted burdens as children. Feelings of rejection in childhood come from derogatory statements *or* from the absence of physical or verbal affirmation. When you're rejected as a child, you're more sensitive to hurt and discouragement as an adult.

Ted grew up in a home where everybody was work-oriented, exhibiting no emotional closeness or physical affection. Ted's parents were busy with their own lives and showed very little interest in him or his accomplishments at school. In his teens, Ted began to wonder why his family wasn't close to him and why no one took much interest in him. His parents weren't mean or abusive. They were polite and courteous, but sterile in their responses. Ted said:

I never could understand why they were so distant. We were together as a family, but it felt like we were miles apart. And then I began to wonder if there was something wrong with me. I felt like I was a burden even though they always provided for me. They never said I was a burden—but I felt that way.

Because of my childhood experience, I've always been fairly cautious about getting close to someone. Maybe there is something wrong with me, and I just can't see it. Sometimes I have daydreams and night dreams about others rejecting me. In my relationships with women, I'm very cautious about getting involved. I'm afraid they will do what my parents did—ignore me. To me, being ignored hurts the same as someone telling me, "You stink. You're no good. I don't like you, and I don't want you." My folks never said those words exactly, but their actions made me feel as though they had.

If I meet a woman I'm interested in, I begin to wonder, "Will she really like me or want me?" I would rather wait for a woman to show an interest in me and pursue me. That's safer. I don't like to pursue them, because if they turn me down, I feel like I've lost a part of who I am. Rejection brings up all those adolescent feelings I had at home. I wish I wasn't this cautious.

Our fear of rejection can be sparked by a childhood sibling, schoolmate, and peer encounter, as described by Lloyd Ogilvie:

> For some it began with an aching suspicion that their parents favored one sibling over another. Others, who didn't battle with the tensions of sibling rivalry, still may not have experienced much esteem-building affirmation of their parents.
>
> Many felt rejection when they did not "measure up" athletically. It was painful to be the last one chosen for a ball team or not chosen at all. Think of the times you were not accepted by the "in" group of kids in the neighborhood or at school. I can remember my first infatuation and the pain of discovering that my "heartthrob" didn't even know I existed.
>
> Who can forget the longing to be popular? Maybe there were times you stood with wallflower anticipation at a school dance or wondered if you would have a date for the prom?

Added to all this may have been the fear of failure in school and the sense of rejection when you didn't quite make the grade. Pressure from parents or competition from our peers can make a poor grade seem like a rejection slip from life.[4]

What About You?

Are you aware of your own feelings of rejection? How deep are they? Take a moment to think about your own feelings of rejection by answering these questions:

- When in your life have you been rejected?
- Describe your feelings of being rejected.
- How have these rejections affected you?
- Is there any way in which you reject yourself?

Did that last question throw you? If you've experienced enough rejection in your life, your fear of being rejected again will cause you to behave in ways that bring about rejection. And many people are so down on themselves that they become their own worst enemies. They put themselves down, degrade themselves, dump on themselves, and rarely give themselves the benefit of the doubt. And because they don't like themselves, they project a negative picture of who they are to others. They operate on the false belief that "because I don't like me, no one else could possibly like me either." They won't *hope* that acceptance will ever happen.

Those who live with this fear are sometimes described by others as being overly sensitive, overly cautious, or overly starved for acceptance. You've met people like this. So have I. And at times in our lives, perhaps we've been there, too.

A Vicious Cycle

Consider how the fear of rejection causes us to respond to life. Mary was a very sensitive person who had experienced rejection in her childhood home and in some of her relationships with men. As we talked together, she revealed the extent of her feelings:

I don't like the way I am. I'm overly sensitive. When I made the appointment with you, I even wondered if you would accept me as a client. Then when I arrived this morning and you were three minutes late for my appointment, those old feelings of rejection began to climb to the surface. It wasn't you but my own sensitivity. I feel that way whenever someone changes plans with me or disagrees with what I think or want. Any time someone doesn't go along with what I want, I begin to feel rejected. And then I get angry inside.

When I'm dating a man and I care for him, I'm even more sensitive to any sign of rejection. But when I feel rejected, I come on too strong and demand love and acceptance in some way. And that chases him right out the door! When that happens, I feel terrible. And I know I caused the rejection. But I don't know what to do!

That's not the only way I respond to my fear of rejection. Sometimes I feel real inhibited with a man, so I withdraw. I'm afraid of exposing my true self and being rejected. But my withdrawal also brings on rejection because he sees me as a real dud. I can't let him know that I care for him and crave his attention and acceptance. So I don't get in. And once again, I get mad! It's almost as if I'm caught in a vicious cycle.

But I don't know how to get out of it!

Mary's right: It *is* a vicious cycle. And it's common. People who live with the fear of rejection have an excessive need for acceptance by others, but they believe and behave in ways that prevent them from experiencing acceptance. They're either so timid, restrained, and closed that no one can get in, or so demanding that they drive others away. In either case, they are rejected because most people don't respond well to either the withdrawal or the demands.

Feelings of rejection breed anger and even rage, but angry feelings are not usually expressed directly because they would bring about more rejection. And so the fear intensifies, which causes the person to need even more acceptance and reassurance, which causes him to respond at even deeper levels of withdrawal or demand. The vicious cycle continues and continues. The same protective devices we created to exorcise rejection from our lives only create more fear and rejection. In time, after multiple rejections our discouragement shifts to depression.

This is why I ask those who are depressed to think back over their lives and identify the rejections they've experienced. These are losses, and if we don't grieve over them, they continue to impact our lives either through fear or depression.

Addicted to Approval

The fear of rejection can also cause us to compromise who we really are. Some have even become *approval addicts.* Underneath their fear of rejection is the misbelief that it is terrible if someone disapproves of them. And underlying this misbelief is some faulty reasoning, "If someone disapproves of me, there must be something wrong with me, and this defect will cause others to disapprove of me as well."

This is a high price to pay for addiction to the approval and acceptance of others. The price tag includes vulnerability to the subjective opinions of the people around you. Others can take advantage of your vulnerability and mistreat you, which leads to additional rejection.

Another false belief held by approval addicts is, "If I'm accepted by others and not rejected, I'll be satisfied and happy. My life will be fulfilled." But no experience of approval leads to permanent satisfaction. Every acceptance "fix" soon wears off, and the fear of rejection returns with a stronger craving for approval.

In reality, we all have varied needs for approval, and the intensity of these needs fluctuates. We may handle some rejections quite well, but some—especially rejection from those significant to us—can crush and devastate. Don't be fooled into thinking that you can gain the approval of everyone.

People-Pleasers

The fear of rejection causes us to become people-pleasers, to call attention to ourselves, or to act inappropriately or awkwardly.

In so doing we set ourselves up for rejection. We become tied to the need that drives us toward others. We develop anxiety about confronting people. We fear expressing an unpopular or different idea that could elicit a conflict of opinion.

The people-pleaser response—also called a compliance compulsion—is quite prevalent. I see this pattern in my counseling practice more and more, especially in wives. Perhaps this accounts for the popularity of a book entitled *The Pleasers* by Kevin Leman.

For people who please, the anger and rage that build up from repeated compromises and rejections finally seek expression. Many people-pleasers who come to me realize there must be a better way to respond to rejection than they now practice. The people-pleaser response is often seen in the "good person." This individual acts friendly, is compliant, and gives out favors left and right to ensure acceptance. But the fulfillment of this person's own needs is denied, because a good person seeking acceptance has little time left for himself.

Elizabeth Skoglund describes the struggle in this way:

Sometimes we try so hard to be accepted that we try to please everyone, an effort which is not only futile but which leaves us with feelings of self-rejection because we have not been true to what we really believe. For ultimately it is not rejection which makes us feel the most pain, but rather what we feel about that rejection and about ourselves. When we choose a course which we know to be right before God, rejection for that choice will hurt but it will not destroy us or our self-image.[5]

Shy and Timid

Fear of rejection may also cause people to appear shy, timid, or ill at ease around others. These people seem to dodge close relationships, some of them commenting, "Who needs other people?" But this attitude can often be translated, "I'm afraid of being rejected." Others may appear cool, aloof, superior, distant, or indifferent. Underlying all this is a sense of discouragement or depression.

A shy person subconsciously expects to be rejected when reaching out. His or her behavior says, *Those people out there are to be feared. They could hurt me. They may not like me. Who would be interested in me? I'm not very sharp, and I can't communicate like others. Anyway, people who would like me must have something wrong with them. They wouldn't be worth getting involved with anyway. I'm not going to say anything. I'll just make a jerk of myself.* Did you notice the negative self-talk? Unfortunately, every crippling statement becomes a self-fulfilling prophecy.

There are a number of false beliefs shy people hold onto as the basis for their fear of rejection. Those who withdraw and appear shy often give these reasons for their manner:

- "I've got to make a good, positive first impression. If I don't they'll never like me or accept me." (This translates to their being slow to speak, and their hesitancy may make the initial impression a disaster.)
- "I *must* be clear and articulate. Otherwise, I shouldn't even try to express myself."
- "I *must* know how to initiate conversation with others in all situations."
- "I *need* to have the perfect opening line." (This belief is

sure to distract shy people from ever opening their mouths. There *is* no perfect opening line!)

- "I *must* be comfortable and fully at ease before I engage others in conversation. Otherwise, they'll notice my discomfort and reject me."

Another misbelief some shy people hold has been called "the myth of the rescuer." They hope that somewhere in the world there is an individual who will rescue them from their relationships, take care of them, and protect them from all rejection. But, of course, the myth of the rescuer is exactly that—a myth.[6]

Wrap-Up

If we end up taking disapproval and other people's opinions of ourselves—their intentional or unintentional disregard—personally, we may begin to expect that we will be blamed by others. And then we get so used to it that we begin to blame ourselves. We've all been rejected in one way or another.

Even Jesus experienced rejection. Isaiah the prophet told of Christ's rejection when he said, "He was despised and rejected by men, a man of sorrows, and familiar with suffering" (Is 53:3). He was rejected by the leaders of Israel and denied and betrayed by others.

And we'll all be rejected in the future in some way. It's a part of life. We can't live the rest of our lives trying to avoid it. If we do, we become prisoners to our fear. And that's no way to live. It's better to face it and learn to overcome it. That's what the next chapter is about.

Chapter 3

Overcoming Rejection

We've identified the problem all right, but now we turn to the big question: "What do I do about my fear of rejection?"

There is hope. Your fear of rejection can diminish or can ultimately vanish. It is possible, especially when your hope is in the person of Jesus Christ. That's how we begin to overcome both the effects of rejection and the fear of rejection. We need to tap into the ultimate source of acceptance.

God's Acceptance

Do you realize how much God accepts you? God sees you as worthy of the precious blood of his Son. Consider the following verses that tell us so:

> Do you not know that your body is a temple of the Holy Spirit, who is in you, whom you have received from God? You are not your own; you were bought at a price. Therefore honor God with your body.
>
> 1 CORINTHIANS 6:19-20

> For you know that it was not with perishable things such as silver or gold that you were redeemed from the empty

way of life handed down to you from your forefathers, but with the precious blood of Christ, a lamb without blemish or defect.

1 PETER 1:18-19

And they sang a new song [to the Lamb]:
   "You are worthy to take the scroll
      and to open its seals,
   because you were slain,
      and with your blood you purchased men for God
      from every tribe and language and people and nation."

REVELATION 5:9

You were bought with a price; that's how valuable you are. Furthermore, God knows you through and through! He is fully aware of you:

And the Lord said to Moses, "I ... am pleased with you and I know you by name."

EXODUS 33:17

Before I formed you in the womb I knew you, before you were born I set you apart.

JEREMIAH 1:5

I am the good shepherd; I know my sheep and my sheep know me ... and I lay down my life for the sheep.... My sheep listen to my voice; I know them ... and they shall never perish.

JOHN 10:14-15, 27-28

James Packer writes,

> There is tremendous relief in knowing that his love to me is utterly realistic, based at every point on prior knowledge of the worst about me, so that no discovery now can disillusion him about me, in the way I am so often disillusioned about myself, and quench his determination to bless me.... He wants me as his friend, and desires to be a friend, and has given his Son to die for me in order to realize this purpose.[1]

In the days and seasons in which we are at peace with ourselves and not bound by the past, we feel as though we belong. We feel *wanted, desired, accepted,* and *enjoyed.* We feel *worthy:* "I count; I'm good." We also feel competent: "I can do it." These feelings give us our sense of identity.

But our times of feeling complete may be all too infrequent. We must continually remember our roots, our heritage. We are created in the image of God. He wants his work to be complete in us. When we relate to his Son Jesus Christ by faith, we have the potential for inner wholeness (see Col 2:10).

Joseph Cooke offers further encouragement:

> This, then, is the wonder of the Christian message: that God is this kind of God; that he loves with a love that is not turned off by my sins, my failures, my inadequacies, my insignificance. I am not a stranger in a terrifying universe. I am not an anomalous disease crawling on the face of an insignificant speck in the vast emptiness of space. I am not a nameless insect waiting to be crushed

by an impersonal boot. I am not a miserable offender cowering under the glare of an angry deity. I am a man beloved by God himself. I have touched the very heart of the universe, and have found his name to be love. And that love has reached me, not because I have merited God's favor, not because I have anything to boast about, but because of what he is, and because of what Christ has done for me in the Father's name. And I can believe this about God (and therefore about myself) because Christ has come from the Father, and has revealed by his teaching, by his life, by his death, by his very person this is what God is like: He is "full of grace."[2]

Look at Yourself

You have a selective memory that needs to be changed to a new channel. Yes, it's true that you have been rejected by others in the past. But what about the times you have been accepted? They are there! Believe it! Look for them! Moses had to remind the children of Israel about the times God had led them. We too need to be called back to positive memories.

List six examples of times when you were accepted by others:

1. _____
2. _____
3. _____
4. _____
5. _____
6. _____

Another step in dealing with your fear of rejection is to identify and list your misbeliefs about acceptance and rejection. Become aware of both the blatant and subtle messages (see chapter 2) that are directing your responses in life.

Also, before focusing on your fear of rejection from others, consider the ways you reject yourself. Do you make rejecting statements about yourself? Think about it. List some that come to mind:

1. _____
2. _____
3. _____

If you identified some, train yourself to counter each rejecting statement with three positive, affirming statements. Could it be that you see yourself responding to others in such a way that they will reject you? Each time you see yourself responding in a hesitant or inadequate manner, imagine yourself in a healthy, positive manner. Practicing this can make a difference. How you think about yourself, see yourself, and talk about yourself determines what happens in your life.

Circle of Acceptance

In southern Africa, the Bebemba tribe has a fascinating procedure for combating feelings of rejection. Each person in the tribe who acts irresponsibly or unjustly is taken alone to the center of the village. Everyone in the village stops work and gathers in a large circle around the accused. In turn, each person in the tribe—regardless of age—speaks to the individual, recounting aloud the good things he has done in his lifetime.

All the positive incidents in the person's life, plus his good attributes, strengths, and kindnesses, are recalled with accurate detail. Not one word about his irresponsible or antisocial behavior is shared.

The ceremony, which sometimes lasts several days, isn't complete until every positive expression has been given by those assembled. At the conclusion of the ceremony, the person is welcomed back into the tribe. Can you imagine the flood of feelings during the tribe's welcome? Can you imagine the extent of acceptance he realizes? Can you imagine how you would feel if a group of people affirmed you in this way?

But what about you? Do *you* accept yourself in that way? Do *you* surround yourself with affirming and encouraging responses? If you open your eyes, you can see that God has surrounded you with more responses than you can ever know. Accept yourself and relish God's acceptance. Read and try to grasp how valuable you are:

How we praise God, the Father of our Lord Jesus Christ, who has blessed us with every spiritual blessing in the heavenly realms because we belong to Christ. Long ago, even before he made the world, God loved us and chose us in Christ to be holy and without fault in his eyes. His unchanging plan has always been to adopt us into his own family by bringing us to himself through Jesus Christ. And this gave him great pleasure.

So we praise God for the wonderful kindness he has poured out on us because we belong to his dearly loved Son. He is so rich in kindness that he purchased our freedom through the blood of his Son, and our sins are forgiven.

EPHESIANS 1:3-7, NLT

Practical Principles

Remember: when someone does respond to you in a rejecting manner, that person may simply be having a bad day. Or perhaps that person has misinterpreted your response—or is just a critical, hurting person! It may be somebody else's problem. Or maybe nobody is at fault; the incident that made you feel rejected happened for some unexplained reason. Being rejected doesn't necessarily mean you have done or said something wrong.

If someone shares a valid criticism with you, focus on the criticism and don't interpret it as a rejection. If the criticism is valid, learn and grow from it. Every person is imperfect and inadequate, and we all have room to grow. When there is a criticism, don't respond to it for twenty-four hours. Think about it first.

It may help you to gather more information about those from whom you sense rejection. A bit of background could help you to avoid problems in future encounters.

Sometimes what people tell us is actually true, but it is packaged abrasively. Remember that what people mean to say, what they actually say, and what we hear them say may be three quite different things. Messages do get mixed up, and sometimes we have our own special filter that distorts what was intended. So when you hear a critical, rejecting message, consider that this message could be more about the other person than about you. Try saying to yourself, "He or she could be having a bad day. This is not really about me at all." Often what others say is more about protecting themselves than about rejecting you.[3]

If you're not sure what the speaker is intending you to hear, you might say something like this: "I'd like to consider what you're saying. Could you say that again in a different way and slower, so I'll be able to hear it better?" Or with a positive tone you could say: "I'm interested in knowing what you want from me. Is there something I can do to make the situation better?" When the person responds, listen fully; don't just listen with one ear while you're trying to figure out what you're going to say next. You will be amazed at how this could take the sting out of the interaction. It's all right to consider the speaker's words but to disregard his or her attitude.

When rejection has occurred or may occur, consider this principle: Take what is said seriously but not personally. It's a matter of screening what others say and processing it appropriately.[4]

If you make a mistake that makes you afraid of being rejected, don't anticipate being rejected ahead of time. Balance your feelings by focusing on the numerous times you were successful. See your small mistake in the context of the positive side of your life.

Criticism and rejection from others can upset you only to the extent that you believe the response of the other person. You can let it linger and destroy you, or you can move ahead. Yes, rejection does hurt, and it's uncomfortable. But avoid the hippopotamus response—don't wallow in your feelings of rejection. Refuse to believe that one rejection will lead to others or that your world is falling apart. Instead, take charge of the situation when it occurs, and turn the negative into a positive by responding to it with courage.

When you are rejected, keep in mind that other people have neither the right nor the ability to judge your value and worth as a person. Don't allow the negative responses of others to determine your value. People are not the experts on your worth; God is. I like what David Burns says about approval and disapproval:

It's a fact that approval *feels* good. There's nothing wrong with that: it's only natural and healthy. It is also a fact that disapproval and rejection usually taste bitter and unpleasant. This is human and understandable. But you are swimming in deep, turbulent waters if you continue to believe that approval and disapproval are the proper and ultimate yardsticks with which to measure your worth.[5]

If others do reject you, in your heart and mind give them permission to do so. Your worth is *not* based on their evaluation.

When you live with the fear of rejection, you live with assumptions based on emotions. Your emotions tell you what to believe about events and relationships. They tell you that you will be rejected and that you are rejected. Counter these feelings with facts. Unless you behave in a way that causes you to be rejected, most of the time you won't be rejected. But when you are rejected, don't assume that you are at fault.

I have felt rejection. I have felt the rejection of someone not liking my speaking, my writing, my counseling. I have had my ideas rejected, and I have been personally rejected by other people. I don't like it. In fact, it's so uncomfortable to feel rejected, I've often wondered why anyone would want to continue to tolerate the fear of rejection, which, as we have previously discussed, can become a vicious cycle that fuels more rejection.

Wrap-Up

When you and I feel rejected, we need to remember who accepts us. Amy Carmichael, a missionary to India early in the twentieth century, noted: "Sometimes circumstances are so that we must be misunderstood, we cannot defend ourselves, we lie open to blame, and yet we may know ourselves clear before God—and man—in that particular matter." Commenting on that statement, Lloyd Ogilvie continues:

> The King of our lives knows! If we are to blame, it cannot be hidden from him. And when we are unjustly criticized or condemned, he understands. In either case, he wants to join with us in a majority opinion of two that, no matter what has happened, we have a bright future and can press on without dreading the next rejection.[6]

Could I make one final suggestion? To confront and defeat the fear of rejection, dwell upon positive thought. A few lines Lloyd Ogilvie uses have been very helpful to many. Speak these words aloud every morning and evening for the next month. You will be amazed at the effect:

> You are secure in God's love. Do not surrender your self-worth to the opinions and judgments of others. When you are rejected, do not retaliate; when you are hurt, allow God to heal you. And knowing the pain of rejection, seek to love those who suffer from its anguish.[7]

Chapter 4

Depression—What's It All About?

Depression. It's not particularly a pleasant word. In fact, I don't know anyone who would say that it is pleasant. What comes to mind when you think of the word *depression*? Have you ever thought about the literal meaning of this word? Think about this. What happens when you depress something such as a lever? You move it from where it was to a lower level. The movement from high to low characterizes depression. Energy, self-esteem, mood, and the appetite for life are all lowered. "I feel so low" is a common statement of a depressed person. Your interest in life is gone. Food has lost its good flavor. It's hard to drag yourself out of bed. Taking out the trash is a superhuman effort. Your output is negligible, and your speed has slowed to a crawl.[1]

Ellen McGrath has developed a new perspective on depression, saying there is a *healthy depression* and an *unhealthy depression*. This possibility does shed new light on the issue. Can depression sometimes be healthy?

Healthy depression involves realistic feelings of pain, sadness, disappointment, guilt, or anger. It could stem from a loss, trauma, past issues, or unfair treatment in some way. It's a normal response to the upset you've experienced. It's based on reality. You're still able to function in your daily life, but you're less effective than usual. You feel bad; at times you feel helpless and may even withdraw for a few hours or a day or two. Even though you feel hurt, you still have hope and the expectation that this will change. You may get down on yourself, but any feelings of self-blame are transient. You also learn from this experience.

Is this something you've experienced? Most of us have at one time or another. But what's the difference between this and unhealthy depression? Actually, there's quite a big difference. The words *immobilized* and *feeling damaged* come to mind. The way you feel is based more on distortion or denial of what is occurring, or there's been too much dumped on you for you to cope. Your functioning in all areas is limited: no interest in life, people, or activities. Your eating and sleeping is disturbed and your memory goes. You feel not hope but despair. You're withdrawn for days or months at a time. You feel damaged beyond repair, and you're filled with chronic low self-esteem. You're unproductive to the extent that there is physical and mental deterioration.[2]

It has also been suggested it's best not to think of depression as a disease to be avoided at all costs, but a process that's either productive or unproductive. It's possible for depression to have a purpose and its purpose is to help a person resolve some inner struggle. If the struggle is resolved and the person moves forward, then depression is purposeful.[3]

When experiencing any type of depression, whether it's healthy or unhealthy, it's important to hear its message and take the steps necessary to get needed help. Remember that healthy depression can turn into unhealthy, so listen to it.[4]

What else can be said about depression?

In simple terms, it's often merely a negative emotion due to self-defeating perceptions and appraisals. However, it may also be a sign of serious, even malignant, disease. *Depression* is a term that can describe the "blahs" or the "blues," or it can describe a neurotic or psychotic disorder. Depression can be mild, moderate, or severe. It can be harmless or life threatening. In other words, there are many varieties of depression with various intensities as well as results. (We'll discuss this further in chapter 5.)

Depression can be an inspiration to some creative people, but it can end in suicide for others. Depression can be a disorder or merely a symptom of a disorder. For example, any of the symptoms of stress can be indicative of depression, and any of the symptoms of depression can be indicative of stress or some other specific ailment.

Did you know that depression can be found in babies younger than one year old and in people who have lived more than a hundred years? In some individuals, depression may be readily observed by any layperson; in others, it may so masked that only experts can recognize it.

Standard Causes of Depression

Depression can be caused by physical, mental, emotional, or spiritual problems, or by a combination of these. It can be caused by our self-defeating thinking or by separation from God. Yet it can also result from a shortage or malfunctioning of essential neurotransmitters in the brain.

Standard causes of depression include fatigue, insufficient or improper food, insufficient rest, reaction to medications, glandular imbalance, PMS, hypoglycemia, food allergies, low self-image, a pattern of negative thinking, behavior that contradicts personal values, and postpartum issues. This is why it is so important for anyone who has been depressed for six months or more to obtain a complete physical exam, including a blood panel, from a physician who understands depression.

Seasonal Affective Disorder

Depression can result from major variables in atmospheric pressure or even from lack of sunlight during the late fall and winter. A thirty-one-year-old woman wrote:

> I used to dread the fall. When the leaves dropped, my mood would, too. I'd see the first leaves on the ground and I'd panic, so I couldn't work. I wouldn't want to wake up and I'd start putting on weight. I couldn't help it. Every fall I'd start this cycle that would last all winter. As soon as the days got longer and the green leaves started on the trees, I'd emerge again.... I often wished I was a bear so I could just go hibernate until spring. It seemed very sensible to me, and a lot less stressful than trying to maintain a regular life.[5]

Some joke about the weather affecting our moods. Well, for some people it is no joke. The words you just read describe a form of clinical depression known as seasonal affective disorder (SAD). This disorder is reflected by severe seasonal mood swings. These usually occur in late fall or early winter and last until spring, when the depression lifts. It appears to affect about four times as many men as women, especially those in their twenties and thirties. Those affected become listless and fatigued, sleep more than in the summer, withdraw socially, feel anxious and irritable, and tend to gain weight. If these symptoms occur at least three different times and twice in consecutive years, then SAD is present.

The physical cause may be an underproduction of the hormone melatonin. Some researchers believe the reduced sunlight of winter affects the brain chemistry, because exposure to light lifts the depression. Those with SAD find relief by spending from thirty minutes to five hours a day in front of a special light box. This is not a tanning bed or just more lights. It's a special box containing several fluorescent tubes that give off the full amount of natural light at ten to twenty times the intensity of indoor lighting.[6] (For additional information about SAD see *Winter Blues*, by Norman E. Rosenthal, M.D.)

Manic-Depressive Disorder

One expression of depression, sometimes called the rollercoaster illness, is bipolar or manic-depressive disorder, which involves wide-ranging mood cycles. A person's lows can be very low, and manic highs give the feeling there is nothing he or she cannot accomplish. The person has a euphoric or high feeling, becomes very active, needing little sleep; thoughts race and are disconnected; speech seems frenetic. Unimportant issues or events distract this person, and he or she has inflated thoughts about personal capabilities. Behavior is impulsive and judgment is poor, sometimes leading to excessive spending, sexual acting out, and other problems.

The person may be in this manic pattern for days and weeks, but then it all stops suddenly as the person hits the other side of the mood swing. This is usually an inherited ill-ness, and it continues to recur. It is not a respecter of gender, as it afflicts men and women in the same numbers. Various medications are used to treat this disease, with lithium as the most frequently prescribed. The "high" euphoric feelings plus three or four of the above symptoms need to exist for the symptoms to be classified as bipolar depression.

Spiritual Dryness

Depression can also be tied to a time in life when we are spir-itually dry. Richard Foster described this condition in *Celebration of Discipline:*

> The "dark night" ... is not something bad or destruc-tive.... The purpose of the darkness is not to punish or afflict us. It is to set us free....
>
> What is involved in entering the dark night of the soul? It may be a sense of dryness, depression, even lost-ness. It strips us of overdependence on the emotional life. The notion, often heard today, that such experi-ences can be avoided and that we should live in peace and comfort, joy and celebration, only betrays the fact that much contemporary experience is surface slush. The dark night is one of the ways God brings us to a hush, a stillness, so that he may work an inner transfor-mation upon the soul....
>
> Recognize the dark night for what it is. Be grateful that God is lovingly drawing you away from every dis-traction so that you can see him.[7]

Depression-Prone?

Some personalities seem to be more depression-prone than others. The following is a general description and not everyone with these characteristics is depression-prone.

The susceptible person is vulnerable to loss.... If a person has experienced a significant loss during his (or her) formative years (e.g. death of a parent), the vulnerability to depression is heightened. The susceptible person is also conscientious, responsible, and has a high personal ethic—quick to feel guilt, whether warranted or not. He (or she) may be ambitious, energetic, and competitive in normal spirits. In spite of a tendency to be self-absorbed, he (or she) does care about the feelings of others, sometimes too much so, and may be overly cautious lest he (or she) inadvertently hurt their feelings. He (or she) tends to find himself (or herself) in deep and sometimes overwhelming involvements, and very dependent on those he (or she) loves. He (or she) is inflexible—highly sensitive to anything that would decrease his (or her) self-esteem in his (or her) own eyes or others' eyes. Being rejected is ... especially painful ... his (or her) need for self-control and control over his (or her) environment is strong. He (or she) has difficulty managing his (or her) hostility—he (or she) may not even be aware of his (or her) own anger, and finds it difficult to mobilize his (or her) emotions in his (or her) defense, even when it is justifiable or necessary.[8]

Do you know anyone who might fit this profile?

A Closer Look at Loss

Earlier in this chapter, I briefly mentioned loss as a cause of depression. But any time a major loss occurs in our life depression is a normal response. And life is full of losses.

Life is a blending of loss and gain, loss and acquisition. In nature, loss is the ingredient of growth. A bud is lost when it turns into a beautiful rose. When a plant pushes its way up through the soil, a seed is lost.

Losses can be obvious: losing loved ones through death or divorce, having a car stolen, a house vandalized and robbed. Other losses may not be so obvious: changing jobs, receiving a *B* instead of an *A* in a college course, getting a minimal raise rather than what we had hoped for, moving, getting ill (loss of health), changing a teacher in the middle of a semester, changing from an office with windows to one without, achieving success that involves the loss of a challenge or of relationships with fellow workers, having a son or daughter go off to school, losing an ideal, a dream, or a lifelong goal. Because they may not be easy to recognize, we don't always identify these as losses, which means we may not spend time and energy dealing with them.

Several years ago at a seminar, a woman told me that she and her husband had moved to a new city three years before. Prior to that time, they had lived in the same town for fifteen years. They were deeply involved in their church and had many friends. Their children had been raised there, and they had celebrated each Christmas with the same close family friends.

When they moved, they left all of that behind. The woman's husband started his new job immediately. Yet because of the nature of her profession, she had to start over and rebuild from scratch. For the first two years she experienced significant depression and couldn't figure out why. Finally, in counseling she focused on her family of origin, and the reason became apparent.

As a child, up to the age of five, she had bonded more with her grandmother than with her mother. They were very close, when her grandmother died suddenly. Within weeks, her family moved from town to the country, where the nearest neighbor was a mile away. As she and her therapist talked and the connection became clear, she was able to grieve as she never had over her grandmother and that childhood move. In time, her depression lifted.

Is there a loss in your life you have never really grieved? Give this question some serious thought before reading the next chapter.

Look at Your Family History

More and more research is being conducted on the question of whether depression or a predisposition toward depression can be inherited.

Inherited depression has been defined as sad or bad feelings that occur when biological depressions exist in a family and are passed down to the next generation as an increased vulnerability to both healthy and unhealthy depression. Sometimes this is disguised so well that it is hard to discern. The factors that are the most difficult to identify as depression are biological or genetic or both. The symptoms may come out as addictions, eating disorders, or psychosomatic disorders.

The tendency to depression can also be passed down by example, as people learn by example and observation. Relatives can pass down depressive ways of thinking and even behaving.[9]

Remember that you may encounter resistance or reluctance to talk about issues such as this. Most of us have never really considered looking at our family trees to determine who was depressed and who wasn't. Some families do not like to bring up the past or reveal what they consider to be family secrets.

I suggest you make a list of family members and try to answer the following questions:

- Was the relative immobilized from time to time and unable to get out of bed, frequently irritable or withdrawn, and often unresponsive? Did this person blame others for his or her bad feelings?
- Was this person frequently "ill" and immobilized with vague explanations as to what the problem was?
- Was economic deprivation a way of life?
- Did the person have accidents, injuries, or fall a great deal?
- Was this person described by others as having bad nerves, a neurotic condition, a melancholic disposition, or a drinking problem?

Positive answers could indicate what we more openly describe today as depression.

As best as you can, rate each of the family members you have listed on a scale of 1 to 10 for his or her level of depression. Use 1 for no depression or minimal depression, 2 to 5 for increasing degrees of healthy depression, and 6 to 10 for increasing degrees of unhealthy depression.

While you're at it, ask yourself where *you* would fall on this scale currently. Five years ago. As an adolescent. As a child. How much change, loss, stress, disappointment, physical illness, or trauma have you experienced in the past two years? In the last year? How have you responded to each situation? What type of support did you experience from others? Was there any anger associated with any of the events? If so, what did you do with it? Was it converted into depression?

How likely is it that depression will have an impact on your life? If you are a woman, you have at least a one-in-four chance of experiencing a major unhealthy depression.[10] If your relatives, especially women, experienced severe neurotic depression or manic depression, you are two to three times more likely than other women to experience these depressions as well. In manic depression there seems to be a depression gene or genes, which could be inherited from either parent.[11]

If there are depression symptoms such as alcoholism or drug abuse among close relatives, you are eight to ten times more likely to develop similar symptoms. If a close relative committed suicide, you will be more vulnerable to suicide if you experience depression.[12]

We still have to face the impact of divorce upon families. This is another factor that contributes to depression even when it was the best option available. As you look at your family tree, try to discover who divorced and when.[13]

If you are depressed in any way, continue to learn as much as you can about it. This book is not the last word on the subject. But I hope it will provide you with some clues, some understanding, some basics, some solutions, and some hope.

Chapter 5

Myths About Depression

Janice sat in my office, looking at the floor. It took her awhile before she spoke. Finally she said, "I've been struggling with depression for so long. I've wanted to do something about it for months, but I was afraid to talk to anyone about it. I'm a Christian. How can a Christian be depressed? I don't know what's wrong with me, what I've done to bring this on, or even if I can get over it. If I were a stronger person, I could get rid of it. I guess I'm just weak. I'm not even sure counseling will do any good. And I definitely don't want to take any medication!"

Janice was struggling like so many do when their lives have been invaded by depression. It's difficult to know what to do and where to turn. And unfortunately, depression often carries with it a stigma of shame that feeds its intensity, especially for a Christian. This stigma can prevent the seventeen million Americans who suffer depression from looking for the help they desperately need. It's estimated that two-thirds of depressed people never get help that would set them on a road to emotional health.

What keeps people from getting the help they need? Often it's a series of myths that are perpetuated by people who are afraid of facing depression (their own and others) and self-proclaimed experts who have little knowledge and understanding.

Let's look at some of these myths and discuss why they are not valid.

Myth 1: Depression for a Christian Is a Sin

In and of itself depression certainly isn't a sin.

Many people are surprised to read the account of Jesus' depression in the Garden of Gethsemane. Jesus was a perfect man and free from all sin, yet complete in his humanity and tempted as we are. Look at the account in Matthew 26:36-38 (AMPLIFIED):

> Then Jesus went with them to a place called Gethsemane, and he told his disciples, "Sit down here, while I go over yonder and pray." And taking with him Peter and the two sons of Zebedee, he began to show grief and distress of mind and was deeply depressed. Then he said to them, "My soul is very sad and deeply grieved, so that I am almost dying of sorrow. Stay here and keep awake and watch with me."

Jesus knew what was about to happen to him, and it caused him to be depressed. He did not feel guilty over being depressed, and neither should we. But our depression creates a distortion of life and intensifies any guilt feelings we have. So guilt over depression leads to more depression.

It's true that some causes of depression can be traced to sinful behavior or thoughts. When our behavior is in conflict with our Christian value systems, the results can be guilt and depression. Depression is a sign to us that a change is needed.

It's a symptom that something in life is amiss. It's like a dashboard warning light that's come on. If you ignore that warning light, your car may stop. If you ignore your depression and don't get the help you need—whether it is to grieve a loss or deal with a sin—there are negative results.

Think of depression as pain caused by a tooth that's decaying. We don't like the pain, but it alerts us and gets our attention. If you didn't feel that pain, eventually you would lose that tooth. Just as tooth pain is not punishment from God, neither is depression a punishment. If anything, depression is a gift in that it warns us that we need to take action to deal with the cause of our depression. Without the "warning," we'd be in worse shape.

Myth 2: Depression Is the Same for Every Person

Not true. Depression varies widely in terms of its severity, symptoms, and causes. Let's walk through several levels of severity or stages of depression.

Perhaps you remember the story of the frog and the boiling water. If you drop a frog into a pan of cool water on the stove, the frog swims about, enjoying itself. But if you turn on the flame under the pan and gradually warm the water, the frog does not sense the change in temperature. He adjusts to the water as the temperature changes. In time the water steams, then boils, and finally the frog is cooked. But the heat comes so gradually and subtly that the frog doesn't realize what is happening until it is too late.

Depression is like that: It is often difficult to detect in its early stages. We may experience some of the symptoms but not understand what they are until they intensify. And when we have moved deeper into depression, it is much more difficult to break its hold. Notice the three stages of depression described below.

Three Intensities of Depression

Light Depression

- Low mood
- Minor loss of interest in life activities
- Thinking processes normal
- Knot in stomach
- Undisturbed eating and sleeping patterns
- Slight spiritual withdrawal

Medium Depression

- Negative symptoms of "light" depression intensified
- Feelings of hopelessness
- Painful and slow thinking processes
- Preoccupation with self
- Self-blame
- Slightly disturbed eating and sleeping patterns

Heavy Depression

- Previous negative symptoms very intensified
- Spiritual withdrawal or obsessive preoccupation
- Neglected personal appearance

Light Depression

Your mood may be a bit low or down. There is a slight loss of interest in what you normally enjoy. A few feelings of discouragement may also be present, but your thinking is still normal. There might be a few physical symptoms, but your sleeping and eating habits remain normal. There may be a slight spiritual withdrawal at times; God may feel far away; you may not be interested in God or your spiritual community.

If you can recognize these symptoms as indications of depression (and if this is a reactionary depression, in response to circumstances and environment), you are still in a position to reverse the depression. Ask yourself these questions:

- What is my depression trying to tell me?
- What may be causing this reaction?
- Would sharing this with another person help? If so, with whom will I talk?
- What Scriptures would be helpful to read at this time, or what other resource would be helpful? (Having a pre-planned reading program in mind will be beneficial. This can include a devotional book and specific passages of Scripture.)
- What type of behaviors or activities would help me at this time?

To keep from going into medium or heavy depression, it is vital that we "let go" of our depression. Letting go before being dragged down into the depths is the key to thwarting long-lasting and heavy depression.

To illustrate this point, imagine that you are in a pool of deep water and holding a heavy rock. The weight of the rock pulls you down. *I'm sinking,* you say to yourself. What does the thought do to you? It makes you feel even worse. All you are aware of now is the fact that you are sinking. In time the surface of the water is over your head. You continue to sink lower and lower and you think, *I'm going down and down and down.* This makes you feel worse, which makes you hold onto the rock even tighter and sink lower, and the vicious circle of thinking and clutching repeats itself.

Is the problem the fact that you are sinking? No! It is the rock. Let go of the rock, and then you'll have the opportunity to begin the journey back up to the surface.

Or perhaps you're swimming, and you discover that you're a little more tired than you thought, or that the water is deeper and the current swifter than you expected. By taking action immediately, you can quickly head for shore and avert a possible disaster. One hopes you'll learn something from the experience. You can take similar action when you are in the light stage of depression.

But if the current is too strong or if you're totally exhausted and on the verge of drowning, you will need the help of a lifeguard. If you are already in the medium or heavy stage of depression, or if your depression has immobilized you and you feel helpless, you need the help of someone who is loving, firm, empathic, and a good listener to help pull you out.

Medium Depression
All of the negative symptoms of light depression will be intensified, with an emerging and prevailing feeling of hopelessness. Thinking is a bit slow, as thoughts about yourself intensify. Tears may flow for no apparent reason. Sleeping and eating problems may emerge—either too much or too little. You sense a greater spiritual struggle, as you retreat from God. To handle this type of depression, you will probably need the

assistance of someone else. But you may resist talking about your difficulty with anyone else. This just intensifies your dilemma.

Severe Depression

All of the previous symptoms occur with great intensity. Personal neglect is obvious—cleanliness, neatness, shaving, or makeup is ignored. A severely depressed person finds it a chore to complete daily tasks. Spiritual symptoms may be evident as either withdrawal from God and community or preoccupation with (and worry about) a relationship with God. A person may cry frequently and feel intense dejection, rejection, discouragement, self-blame, self-pity, and guilt. Patterns of eating and sleeping are disrupted.

Some readers may find the following list helpful in identifying a *major depressive episode*. Here that term is defined by a person exhibiting at least five of the following symptoms every day for five weeks. Here are the symptoms:

1. You feel depressed or in an irritable mood most of your day. (It's easy to associate irritability with anger.)
2. Your interest or pleasure in either all or most of your activities has taken a nosedive. It's just not there anymore.
3. Your sleeping habits have changed—it's either insomnia or excessive sleep.
4. The way in which you do things or move could either be agitated or retarded.
5. Your energy is gone and fatigue is your companion.
6. You either gain or lose weight, your appetite either grows or goes.
7. You feel worthless or guilty (excessive or inappropriate).

8. You're not as sharp mentally—concentration is diminished and or indecisive.

9. You have recurrent thoughts of death or even suicidal thoughts or even a specific plan for the latter.[1]

If this is a description of you, I suggest you seek professional counseling from a therapist who is knowledgeable in the field of depression. To find names of therapists in your area, call Focus on the Family (719-531-3400) or the American Association of Christian Counselors (800-526-8673).

Depression obviously covers a wide spectrum in terms of its stages or strength of force. Chapter four discussed various aspects of depression, but it's always helpful to remember that depression can be linked to specific medical issues.

It could be the result of alcoholism.

It could be a side-effect of blood pressure medication or birth control pills.

It could be tied into hepatitis, multiple sclerosis, Parkinson's disease, or childbirth.

It could be a symptom of a viral infection, AIDS, chronic fatigue syndrome, and so forth.

Causes are complex, and the symptoms vary in terms of intensity and manifestation.[2] Not all depression is the same.

Myth 3: If I Had Enough Willpower,
I Could Overcome My Depression

If you are beyond the light stage of depression and if you believe or others tell you that if you had enough fortitude and character you could overcome your depression, don't believe this. All this does is reinforce the negative thoughts you already have about yourself. Belief in this myth can lead a depressed person to label herself as weak, stupid, defective, or a failure.

All of us will have negative thoughts from time to time, and we can correct them. But a depressed person has a hard time breaking the hold of negative thoughts. A depressed person is riding an emotional roller coaster. He's not the driver and cannot stop and go at will. This coaster just keeps going and going.

Remember, willpower is not a treatment method for depression. You don't heal an illness that has biological, social, psychological, and genetic components with willpower.

Myth 4: If I'm Depressed, I Can't Be Productive

Many who are depressed and are receiving treatment lead very productive lives. They are able to carry out work, social, church, and family responsibilities. In fact, in many cases carrying out these responsibilities is what keeps the people going. Being productive encourages their hopeful outlook.

Myth 5: Counseling Won't Work

In 80 percent of the cases, therapy for depression is effective. Research shows there is no better approach than psychotherapy in the treatment of depression, whether it's a mild case or severe. One of the largest surveys ever conducted on the use of therapy, medication, or both to treat depression (four thousand subscribers to *Consumer Reports*) indicated that therapy by itself worked as well as therapy combined with drugs such as Prozac or Xanax. Sometimes, though, therapy by itself is not sufficient and medication is very beneficial.

Myth 5: If I Take a Medication, I'll Become Addicted to or Dependent on It

Some are afraid that if they begin using a prescribed drug, they will need more and more of it to obtain results. And some are also afraid of overdoing and becoming dependent upon the medication forever. Actually neither of these conditions occur with most of our present-day medications, if they are taken as directed.

Some, such as people with a bipolar condition, may need to take medication for the rest of their lives. But this is something one can be thankful for, that such a medication can bring a balance into life.

Medication is typically used for *severely* depressed individuals but usually in conjunction with therapy. Do you know why the two are used together? Each benefits the use of the other. The medication puts someone in a frame of mind that allows therapy to be more helpful. And the therapy puts that person in a frame of mind that helps him or her stick to a medication schedule.

Medication is beneficial to 70 to 80 percent of those who use it. If there's a problem, it's that only about one-third of the people who could benefit from it ever use it. Most people don't understand how medication helps a depressed individual. It's quite simple actually. Depression often involves imbalances in certain brain chemicals called neurotransmitters (for example, serotonin and norepinephrine), which are needed to transmit messages from one nerve cell to another. The medication is used to bring things back into balance. Medications are corrective, not addictive. They alleviate the disturbing symptoms of depression, such as pessimism, suicidal thoughts, insomnia, anxiety, sensitivity to rejection, apathy, and lethargy.

Beware of the people who recount to you the stories of Uncle Fred or Cousin Mabel who took medication and went crazy or couldn't breathe or never had sex again. They'll try to talk you out of what you're taking. Their examples are usually unfactual, embellished, or extreme, and there are usually other factors that can explain what purportedly occurred. If someone approaches you in this way, I suggest you ask what courses he has taken in the field of pharmacology, what pharmacological books she has read, or whether he is a pharmacist or a medical doctor. The person will probably say, "No, but...." You can then say you've made your point and move on to something else. Self-appointed experts in this area should not be left unchallenged, lest they continue to interfere in the lives of others. Your responses (or those of someone else who is nearby to help you) can save others from grief.

Remember, only a physician, psychiatrist, psychopharmacologist, or biopsychiatrist can make decisions in this area.

Accept the Challenge

I've given a lot of information in chapters four and five. Before we continue, I challenge you to fight a war against depression in your life. As I've said, willpower will not cure depression, but a willingness to let go of pain and reach for help is itself a form of *fight* that can help you overcome.

Remember this about depression:

Fighting depression is war. The best ammunition we have is the knowledge that we will probably win the fight. Depression often retreats on its own if given enough time. The miserable feelings, the hopelessness, and the agony will leave. But if the depression doesn't leave on its own, there are many treatment options.

The knowledge that you will win over depression should be reassuring, but don't be naïve about the enemy. Depression is powerful. Left unchallenged, it can cause a lot of damage.[3]

If you don't fight it depression will make you miserable. Many depressive episodes last between three and twelve months. If you really don't want to be miserable that long, you have to fight. Here are some reasons why you should fight.

Depression impairs judgment. Any depressed person's thinking patterns will be distorted. Consequently, you may make disastrous mistakes while depressed—even quit your job or walk out of your marriage. When the depression lifts, you look back and think, *How could I have done such a thing?* Not to fight depression is to take a chance on doing something you'll regret later.

Depression sets a person up for unnecessary hurt. Feeling bad turns to a magnet that attracts more hurt. A depressed person has a lessened ability to cope and be flexible; your actions won't be what they should be. Or this phenomenon could occur on an unconscious level. You unconsciously set yourself up to prove how awful you are or how bad your situation is. Either way, the result is unnecessary and often hard-to-forget emotional pain. Fight it early on.

Depression intensifies a person's sense of helplessness, especially in women. If you are depressed due to learned helplessness, a failure to fight the illness contributes to your sense of helplessness. You may end up seeing your depression as one more thing over which you have no control.

Depression leads to a feeling of hopelessness. If you are experiencing this, what do you remember? In moments of suffering, all the good moments are blotted out. This would be bearable if you had the conviction that things would eventually improve. But hopelessness makes you think things will never improve. The earlier you fight the illness, the sooner you will begin to feel better. As with other illnesses, the longer you wait before treating it, the more difficult it can be to treat.[4]

Depression experts talk in terms of a kindling effect. An initial episode of depression appears in response to a severe stressful event. The next time the event doesn't have to be quite as severe to ignite a depressive episode. As time goes on, it takes less and less to send the sufferer into an emotional tailspin. Fighting depression thwarts its power for recurrence.

Depression is a powerful enemy we should never underestimate. Fortunately, many weapons are available for fighting this illness. Some of these weapons are stored in our arsenal; others are available through professionals.[5]

Chapter 6

The Blue Mood

Let's take a closer look at what some call the "blue mood." It's not the same as a major clinical depression. You don't have as many problems and the ones you have are not as severe, but the blue mood, or low-grade depression, is still a depression. It's possible to overcome this problem, but it's also possible to sustain it. Not many I know want to purposely sustain it, but inadvertently lots of people end up doing just that.

Self-Evaluation

How do you know if you have the blues? These three questions provide the key:

- Do you feel blue, out of sorts, sad, irritable most of the day? Do you feel gloomy and joyless?
- Are most of your days like this?
- Think about the past two years. Have you had times when you were free from the blues? Did these times last less than two months?

Affirmative answers to these questions may confirm a blue mood. There are many variations. One person may feel empty and another irritable and complaining. Some may sit in silent self-pity; others may verbally dump all over themselves. Some seem always down; others come back to normalcy now and then.

The fancy word for the blue mood is *dysthymia*. Let's get even more specific about its characteristics to see if this is really you (or someone you know). The closer you are to a 10, the more the blue mood could be part of your life.

1. What's going on with your appetite? Has it disappeared or awakened with a vengeance? For some people, buying, preparing food, and eating is a chore. Even if that is true for you, you neither reduce your intake nor lose weight. Many do just the opposite. You look for food and especially sweets.

   0————————————5————————————10
   Not at all   Average   This is me!

2. Sleep disturbances are common. Your body's internal time clock has its wires crossed. You don't get the rest you need. You sleep too much or have insomnia. Your sleep is restless, you wake up early and no matter what you try you can't get back to sleep, or you are plagued by nightmares.

   0————————————5————————————10
   Not at all   Average   This is me!

3. You have low energy and are excessively tired. The lack of motivation and fatigue is not the lethargy experienced in a major depression, but it's still a problem.

   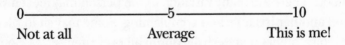

   0————————————5————————————10
   Not at all   Average   This is me!

4. There is a mental aspect to this as well. Someone with the blues thinks slowly. What you used to understand quickly takes longer to figure out or recall. You find yourself distracted. Some people are this way normally (it's a personality trait), but for others this is a change from their typical reactions.

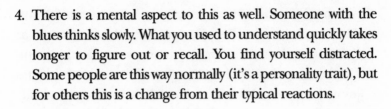

```
0————————————————5————————————10
Not at all              Average        This is me!
```

5. Your feelings about yourself are negative and confidence is low. Because of self-criticism you assume that others see you this way, and you may interpret others' responses to fit your preconceived ideas. You hear negative responses where they don't exist.

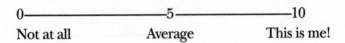

```
0————————————————5————————————10
Not at all              Average        This is me!
```

6. Another characteristic is the feeling of helplessness. Tomorrow won't and can't get better. It will either be like today or worse. And there's nothing you can do about it.

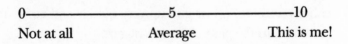

```
0————————————————5————————————10
Not at all              Average        This is me!
```

There are additional symptoms. Numerous people have identified with some of the following.

7. You lose interest in what used to be amusing and fun for you. What used to be enjoyable no longer is. Jokes lose their humor. You even wonder, *Why did I ever laugh at that?*

Accomplishments no longer give a sense of satisfaction. There's a loss of joy. People experience this in burnout as well. I went through a burnout twenty years ago. I remember that scary feeling, knowing that what used to bring me joy no longer did. What I used to delight in doing I basically couldn't care less about. I did not like that feeling.

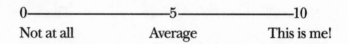

0————————————5————————————10
Not at all   Average   This is me!

8. You feel increased anxiety and fear about any and all future events. The "what ifs ..." creep into your life. Whatever you can find to worry about, you do. It's as though your brain got stuck on a track of negative preimaging the future, and you can't find the switch to turn it off. The key word is *rumination.* It just keeps on going and going and going, like the Energizer Bunny.

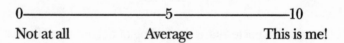

0————————————5————————————10
Not at all   Average   This is me!

9. You're also less productive than previously. This is exhibited in many ways. It takes longer to do even the routine. You either put things off or give up very quickly and easily. You move toward the path of least resistance.

You have to spur yourself to get yourself to complete the routine tasks of everyday living. And even if you complete them, you don't have much of a sense of accomplishment. You end up thinking, *Ah, I could have done it sooner, better, and it won't last.*

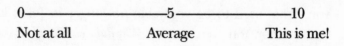

0————————————5————————————10
Not at all   Average   This is me!

10. You are more aware of problems with people, either in reality or in your thinking about them. You feel taken advantage of. No one really cares about what you think. It'd be great if others would do what you ask (and you think they don't) and let you alone when you say no instead of making you feel guilty. About 50 percent of those with the blues struggle with this. It's the result of not knowing how to get what you want, but because of the blues you don't believe it will ever change. If you're a submissive or people-pleasing person to begin with, it's even worse.

```
0———————————————5———————————————10
Not at all            Average            This is me!
```

11. When life is colored by a blue mood, you end up believing that you have no influence on your life whatsoever. You're at the mercy of God, gods, fate, the stars, the tide.... Something outside your life is running your life for reasons that are beyond you.

```
0———————————————5———————————————10
Not at all            Average            This is me!
```

12. The blue mood interferes in another critical area as well: building relationships. You may be a gregarious, outgoing person by nature, but when this mood hits, you become just the opposite. You may even withdraw from the people and activities that once delighted you. If you're married, conflicts may arise because of this; I've seen more than one romantic relationship deteriorate because of this condition.[1]

```
0———————————————5———————————————10
Not at all            Average            This is me!
```

Are you susceptible to the blue mood? A person experiencing any type of depression wonders, *What's going on? It doesn't make sense!* Well, if you're depressed and you're wondering why, you're not alone. Specialists and researchers have been trying to discover the reasons for years. All that has been determined is there are many factors. Some people do seem to be more susceptible to the blues, but it doesn't mean that everyone who experiences these symptoms will experience the blues. Then, to add to this dilemma, many experience the blues who don't have these influences in their lives! Normal blues are occasional and temporary. But a true "blue mood" can go on and on; the mood creeps into our lives slowly and takes up residence. Some underlying family-related factors may make some people more susceptible to depression than others.

A Look at Family Patterns

In chapter four, we discussed looking at family history and depression. This is especially important for anyone with a blue mood. This malady seems to run in families. If you have three or more relatives with this mood, it could be you have a predisposition to the blues. And if either parent was hospitalized for depression or committed suicide, the predisposition is higher. Remember, however, this is a predisposition, not a certainty. If you were around depression much of the time as a child, whether you planned on it or not, you probably learned about it and incorporated it into your life. You didn't have the resources to fight it off.

When we come from an unhealthy family environment our predisposition to depression is enhanced. Dysfunctional families lack much of the acceptance, openness, affirmation, communication, love, caring, and togetherness of healthy families. In most cases, a dysfunctional family is the product of a dysfunctional husband-father, one who failed to occupy a healthy, positive role due to uninvolvement, domination, illness or death, desertion or divorce, and so forth.

Several times a year I travel on airplanes. So far I've always arrived at my intended destination, mainly because the plane stayed on course. If a plane strays off course just a few degrees, I might end up in Cuba instead of Washington, D.C. The longer a plane travels off course, the farther it wanders from its destination.

A dysfunctional family is one that has strayed off course. Though they probably don't think of it in these terms, every newly married couple wants to build a functional family. Their "destination" is a loving, healthy, happy relationship between husband and wife, parents and children. But many little things can go wrong in families: feelings get hurt, needs and expectations go unmet. If these minor midcourse errors are not corrected, greater problems arise: love and acceptance are withheld, "me" and "mine" take priority over "us" and "ours."

Abandonment

One way a father or mother contributes to a dysfunctional family is by abandoning a child. Parents abandon children in numerous ways. Did parents do or exhibit the following to you or to someone you know?

- actually physically leave the child;
- fail to display emotions for the child;
- fail to affirm the child's expressions of emotions;
- fail to provide for the child's developmental dependence needs;

- abuse the child physically, sexually, emotionally, or spiritually;
- use the child to fill the parent's own unmet needs;
- use the child to meet the needs of the parents' marriage;
- deny or hide from the outside world the parents' shameful activities so a child had to cover for them to keep the family in balance;
- completely fail to give a child time, attention, and direction.

When parents abandon a child in one or more of these ways, the natural roles of parents and child are reversed. The parents, through immaturity and irresponsibility, become the children. Having no one to take care of her, the child becomes a parent. She must take care of herself *and* her parents. This unfortunate role reversal leaves many children feeling alone and alienated.[2]

Shame

If you are the product of a dysfunctional family, you probably live with an unhealthy burden of shame. Some of the rules a parent imposed and some of the ways you were abandoned may have left you with a feeling of shame about yourself. Shame is one of the most depressing, disturbing, and deadening responses to life. Shame prevents you from accepting yourself.

Shame flaws the real you so that just trying to be yourself is painful. To survive the pain, you develop a false self, a defensive mask that is used to hide from yourself and others the pain and loneliness you feel. And if you wear the mask long enough, you forget which is the real you—the mask or what's under it. So often, too often, I've heard, "I don't even know who I am. I have no identity." This is more often the cry of women than of men.

The effect of shame is graphically stated by John Bradshaw:

Shame is like a hole in the cup of our soul. Since the child in the adult has insatiable needs, the cup cannot be filled. As grown-ups we can't go back as children and sit in Mom's lap or have Dad take us fishing. And no matter how hard we try to turn our children, lovers, and spouses into Mom and Dad, it never works. We cannot be children again. No matter how many times we fill the cup—the hole remains.

Shame fuels compulsivity and compulsivity is the black plague of our time. We are driven. We want more money, more sex, more food, more booze, more drugs, more adrenalin rush, more entertainment, more possessions, more ecstasy. Like an unending pregnancy, we never reach fruition.

Our diseases are about the things of everyday life. Our troubles are focused on what we eat, what we drink, how we work, how we sleep, how we are intimate, how we have orgasm, how we play, how we worship. We stay so busy and distracted that we never feel how lonely, hurt, mad, and sad we really are.[3]

Shame has often been confused with guilt. John Bradshaw says that there is a significant and profound difference between shame and guilt. Guilt says, "I've done something wrong"; shame says, "There is something wrong with *me.*" Guilt says, "I have made a mistake"; shame says, "*I* am a mistake." Guilt says, "What I did wasn't good"; shame says, "*I* am no good."

Have you entertained any of these feelings of shame? Was shame a prevailing feeling in your relationship with your father?[4]

Remember, a home that *fails* to provide for the basic nurturing of a child is the root of this shame that can feed depression.

Other Factors

There are many who come from healthy homes. So why do some end up experiencing the blues? Life experiences can impact us in many ways. I've seen adults who would prefer to forget their adolescent years. They were not pleasant. It was one adjustment problem after another, many of which included rejection after rejection.

Life is also full of transitions. We enter school, graduate, get a job or get turned down, get married, have children, get new jobs. Do you remember what a transition is? It's moving from one stage of certainty to another stage of certainty with a stage of uncertainty in between. But if you end up with too much uncertainty, your sense of security erodes. And that happens to many.

If a person has experienced numerous losses or crises in life and failed to grieve over them or if the number of losses or crises is overwhelming, that person may well be more susceptible to the blue mood.

Many other issues can contribute to the blues, such as ongoing marital or family conflict, financial problems, parenting, and continuing health issues.[5]

Not only do all these factors contribute to low-grade depression, but if you are depressed, that in itself makes it hard for you to handle these issues.

Having discussed these possible underlying causes, I want to make it clear that you don't *have* to know what's causing the blues to find relief. I've talked with many who have said, "I used to believe I had to know the exact cause before I found relief. But I have some depressed friends who have it all figured out, and it hasn't helped them. I guess what helps me is to know there *are* causes for what I'm experiencing. That in itself is helpful. I may be able to pinpoint the cause. That might happen now or later after I'm over it. Even if I don't, my goal is to get over this. I'll put my efforts in that direction." That's wise.

There are a few other factors to remember about the blues.

Remember that *your* behavior can feed your blues. The way you behave can either encourage or discourage you. It can uplift or drag you down. When you're suffering from the blues, you unfortunately begin to behave in ways that reinforce your depressive feelings and thoughts about yourself. It becomes a vicious circle.

If your behavior isn't purposeful and productive, if you wander through the day with few accomplishments, there will be results, but not the desirable kind.

If you are inactive or nonproductive, you end up with too much time to focus on what is wrong with your life. You can further feed your sense of nonaccomplishment.

When you have the blues, information is processed selectively. Usually you focus on one part of a situation, the most negative one, and then either exaggerate or recount it. You look at life through a negative filter. Sometimes this draws you to sad rather than happy stories, unpleasant rather than pleasant encounters, and a focus on your defects rather than your assets. You're into mental "instant replay" of the worst moments of the day. And any real negative experience is infused with so much power it can erase all memory of positive experiences over the last several days. Positives and future possibilities are put into a dumpster.

Helpful Advice

If what you have been reading about is you, remember, there is hope. You probably don't believe that; you may scoff at it, be offended by it, or think it refers to someone else but not you! I like the approach that Dr. Robert Hirschfeld has taken. He suggests that you take a notebook and write the following on a page:

1. My blue thoughts, feelings, and behaviors are not reversible character flaws. They are symptoms of a treatable illness. People can and do recover from the blue mood.
2. What's done is done. I cannot go back and change the past; however, I can learn to do things differently in the future.
3. Other people are in this predicament. They have a problem, but they also have skills, strengths, talents, and other positive attributes. So do I.
4. As painful as it may feel right now, by recognizing, coming to understand, and acknowledging the problems that chronic blues have caused me, I am taking a step in the right direction—my first step toward recovery.

After you have written these statements, read them to yourself and then aloud. Then read them aloud again with more conviction. They are facts that contradict the inaccurate and unproductive ideas that ran through your mind earlier and that will probably arise again. Return to them as often as you need to. By writing and rewriting, then reading and rereading those facts, you neutralize your discouraging thoughts and become more open to the information you will need in order to overcome the blue mood.[6]

Chapter 7

Triggers That Set Off the Blues

Triggers—we all know about triggers. They're a small part of guns that you pull to set everything in motion. Some triggers require considerable effort to activate. Others are what we call "hair triggers": the slightest pull sets them off.

There are triggers that we pull to set off a blue mood. When the blues hit us, they don't take over just one room in our lives, like the kitchen or bedroom or the dining room; the blues are more like a liquid gas or an oozing foam that spreads throughout an entire structure.

Emotions as Triggers

Our emotions can trigger a blue mood. Not always, of course. Our feelings are normal, natural, and necessary. Sometimes even unpleasant emotions can prompt us to take positive action. I've seen anxiety in a seminary student preparing to present a sermon motivate him to study, rehearse, and practice so that ultimately his level of anxiety dropped and he produced and presented a quality work, better than he would have if he had not been spurred by that anxiety. There is potential in all of our feelings. But if you have the blues, you don't see much value in the emotions you're feeling. Any that are painful, unpleasant, or even just a bit uncomfortable are seen as an enemy or a threatening, controlling force. The best response to emotions is to feel them, face them, express them, learn from them, and try to determine their cause and resolve any problems brought about by them. If you have the blues, though, you'll probably do one of the following.

You may try to avoid any situation that creates the emotion. This could include specific people, places, social events, and doctors' appointments. But unfortunately we may also try to avoid a necessity, a potentially enjoyable experience, a significant accomplishment, or a critical advancement. In the quest to avoid certain emotional responses because they may be painful, we end up bringing about a bigger problem. We end up with feelings that are actually worse than those we were trying to avoid. You could feel more lonely, more lethargic, more disillusioned, and fail to learn through the experience.

Another way of trying to avoid feelings is to bury or numb them. It is possible to put a lid on them and stuff them into a container by using alcohol or drugs or even overeating. With this approach, you can deaden your unpleasant feelings, but you also end up killing your positive feelings. Numbing through these methods will prolong the blues, not help them.

I've seen others who go to the opposite extreme by taking their emotional temperature constantly. They notice every sensation, analyze it, talk about it, talk to themselves about it, and attempt to fix themselves. They're so preoccupied with anything unpleasant that they can't notice positive feelings. It's as if this person is a sentry on the top of a hill trying to note the invasion of the blues again. It's easy to interpret any negative feelings as an out-of-proportion "beginning of the end."

Thirty-year-old Janice did what many do with their feelings.

Her story describes the process:

> Most of the time I feel inept and incapable of really having
> a relationship with anyone. So when overtures occur from
> a man, I like them and want them, but I turn them down.
> If we ever did get together, he'd discover how inept and
> shallow I am, and I couldn't stand the rejection. I even
> turn down promotions at work. If I took the new position,
> I know I couldn't perform satisfactorily, and then they
> would discover I wasn't what they thought I was, and that
> would be unbearable! I guess I lose out on the possibilities,
> but the way I feel about myself is a fact—isn't it?

That's just the problem. It's not a fact. When you have the
blues, you believe that your negative feelings reveal facts, and
you let that rule your life. Your feelings perpetuate the blues.

Any of these responses keeps a person stuck. Feelings aren't
the problem. They don't need to be corrected. Our responses
do, and they can be changed.

Thoughts as Triggers

Another major trigger of the blues is one's thought life. Have
you ever listed the thoughts you have about yourself and your
situation? What you believe and say to yourself can keep you
depressed. In fact, I've seen it bring on depression in a person.
All of us begin to learn from early childhood to formulate
thoughts, perceptions, and feelings in words, phrases, and
sentences. Most of us, by the time we reach adulthood, regu-
late much of our important thinking and consequently our

emotions in terms of our internalized sentences or self-talk. *What people say to themselves governs the way they feel and act!* And we all talk to ourselves. That's normal. But what do we say?

Even emotions, such as anxiety, anger, love, and elation, are often associated with or result from self-talk. Each emotion is determined by the kind of self-talk expressed. Many of our responses have become automatic. Negative thoughts, self-defeating thoughts, and anxiety-creating statements become as automatic and unconscious as driving a car.

Charles Swindoll describes the importance of thoughts in this way:

> Thoughts, positive or negative, grow stronger when fertilized with constant repetition. That may explain why so many who are gloomy and gray stay in that mood, and why others who are cheery and enthusiastic continue to be so, even in the midst of difficult circumstances. Please do not misunderstand. Happiness (like winning) is a matter of right thinking, not intelligence, age, or position. Our performance is directly related to the thoughts we deposit in our memory bank. We can only draw on what we deposit.
>
> What kind of performance would your car deliver if every morning before you left for work you scooped up a handful of dirt and put it in the crankcase? The fine-tuned engine would soon be coughing and sputtering. Ultimately, it would refuse to start. The same is true of your life. Thoughts about yourself and attitudes toward others that are narrow, destructive, and abrasive produce wear and tear on your mental motor. They send you off the road while others drive past.[1]

Characteristics of Automatic Thoughts

Our thoughts jump into our consciousness without any planning or conscious prompting. Consider the characteristics of automatic thoughts.

First of all, an automatic thought is a specific message. A young woman who is afraid of being rejected by men tells herself, "He isn't interested in me. I'm not attractive enough."

Often an automatic thought surfaces not in a complete form but in a shorthand manner, maybe a visual image or just a few words. The automatic thought may be a brief memory of something that happened in the past, or it could be a series of disconnected words. A word or a series of short telegraphic phrases may serve as a label or summary for an entire group of painful memories, fears, or self-degrading statements.

We usually believe our automatic thoughts regardless of how irrational or off the wall they appear. They may appear rational, because we very rarely check them out or verify them. Because they go untested, the more they occur, the more we believe them.

Automatic thoughts are often wound around the terminology of *must, should,* or *ought.* These are called the "torture words," because they elevate guilt and lower self-esteem. "I should do this ..."; "I must be a perfect mother"; "I ought to be consistent and never make a mistake." When these torture words appear on the screen of a person's mind, they generate hopelessness.

Automatic thoughts have a unique characteristic of "awfulizing." They can color our attitudes for days, prompting us to expect the worst, see the danger behind every bush, and be anxious.

Automatic thoughts are also difficult to stop. They may

appear somewhat reasonable, and because they just "pop in," they may become camouflaged among our other thoughts. It's hard to put a leash on them; they tend to come and go at will.

Automatic thoughts are learned. A person listens to others and what they say about him or her and believes those statements.

Feeding the Blues

How do you know if your thinking is nurturing a depressed mood? Several authors have suggested the following.

Your thinking pattern is feeding a depressed mood when it:
- makes it more difficult for you to cope with life experiences, including ordinary, everyday ones like dining alone in a restaurant;
- creates unnecessary confusion, stirring up anxiety or a "hornet's nest" of other emotions;
- causes needless discomfort and inappropriate or extreme reactions, intensifying emotional pain or increasing the stress of already stressful situations;
- leads to self-defeating behavior or prevents you from achieving your goals;
- prompts you to draw the conclusion that "the way things are" is carved in granite, and you are utterly powerless to change them.[2]

Do you identify with any of these patterns? If so, how often do they occur? Weekly? Daily?

If your thoughts feed your blues, it's not as if you purposely want this to happen. Somewhere along the line you've learned this pattern of thinking. Some of your thoughts lurk around for much of the time; others are unwelcome, intermittent visitors. The main problem is equating your thoughts with reality. Too often you think, *I had that thought, therefore, it must be true.* That's why learning to challenge negative thoughts is so important.

Can you think of negative, potentially false statements that you make? What different responses could you make to counter your statements?

A number of years ago the stock market plunged and many lost their savings. That day was referred to as Black Friday. It upset the lives of thousands. There's something else that's black and upsets many lives. It's called black thoughts. Something happens that darkly dominates our thoughts and brings on the blues. We get stuck focusing on these black thoughts and soon our mood reflects the darkness. We weren't called to live in the darkness, but in light. And to allow the light back into our lives, we need to refashion our thoughts and reconstruct our present lives.[3]

There could be many, but let's discuss one culprit that can contribute to the dark thoughts that bring on the blue mood. This may not be your culprit, but for many it is, usually because experiences in their personal histories lean them this direction. Have you ever made negative self-comparisons? You know, giving others the accolades and giving yourself the leftovers? Or giving others the benefit of the doubt and being exceptionally hard on yourself? Sometimes you compare yourself with the way you think things should be, must be, or you want them to be, and they always come up short. A constant diet of this doesn't bring light into your life; it brings discouraging darkness. Once this occurs, another dark thought makes its way into your mind along with all the others, and its purpose is to keep your blue mood locked in place. Your new thought is *I'm helpless and can't change what's going on in my life or my thoughts.* This is called the SS or stuck syndrome.

So when you compare yourself with something that you think should be a certain way but isn't, and you believe you're helpless to change it, your blue mood is in place.[4] Simple statements like, "They get all the breaks," and, "Why don't they show as much interest in what I do?" are set up.

What are your comparisons, and where did they come from? Is it reasonable for a six-year-old to compare himself to an eleven-year-old? No. It isn't fair. Do you judge others with the same measure you use on yourself, or are you harder on yourself? Those with the blues usually are harder on themselves than they are on others. One woman told me that she compared the way she dressed with the way others at church dressed and ended up discouraged. Others seemed to look better and were more stylish. I asked, "Is that good or bad?"

She said, "Well, it's good for them."

"Why does it mean it's bad for you? If you didn't compare but simply looked in a mirror, what would you say about the way you dress?"

Her response was, "Well, I do look all right, I guess."

I asked, "What benefit do you get out of comparing?"

"I guess very little."

"So if you get very little out of it, why do it? Perhaps if you didn't compare, you could give to yourself every positive thought you make about how others dress. Have you ever thought about that?"

She hadn't and for the next week that was her assignment. If you identify with her, perhaps you could take on the same assignment.

There are several steps that you can take. First, identify any negative self-comparisons that you are making. Carry a three-by-five card with you and every time you make a negative comparison, write it down. How does each comparative thought make you feel helpless to change or attain what you want? Rewrite each comparison to give yourself (rather than the other person or the situation) the benefit of the doubt. If you make statements like, "I can't ..."; "I must not ..."; "I'm unable to ..." change each one to the opposite, a positive. This can change your feelings of helplessness and hopelessness to, "Perhaps there is a possibility...."

Second, try to determine where the possible causes of your negative self-comparisons originated. Were you raised in a home of perfectionists? Did you have numerous school experiences in which people were controllers? Did you hear a lot of "shoulds" or "oughts"? Were expectations extremely high, with parents or teachers comparing you to others? You can't change the past. It's futile to try. Yet you can change the effects of the past and rewrite the present and the future.

The third suggestion may seem a bit threatening to some. Consider the queston: Are there any benefits that you are receiving from having a blue mood that could interfere with giving it up? There are some people who really don't want to give it up. And the word *want* is important. Some "want" to get rid of the blue mood but don't want to give up the benefits. It's comparable to "wanting" that extra piece of cream pie, but not "wanting" those extra seven hundred calories around my waistline. In this case, one has a conflict.

How do benefits enter into feeling blue? You know that what you're doing in life (overworking, eating too much, violating moral codes) is creating the blues, but you like or want what you're doing too much to change. There's a conflict. Some people use a mild depression as an excuse to get out of work or responsibilities or to avoid the demands of others or life. Another benefit of the blues is feeling sorry for yourself.[5]

Take a minute to identify any benefits you receive from your blues.

A fourth step involves a direct challenge to your sense of helplessness and hopelessness—the beliefs that take a self-comparison and turn it into the blues; the main ingredient that makes a formula work. Each belief or feeling needs to be challenged.[6] Sometimes I suggest to counselees, "Every time you feel or say you're helpless, that's all right. You can keep that feeling. But for each time it occurs, you need to write down three reasons why it's not true. Do this each day for a week, and let's see what happens." There's quite a change at the end of the week.

Claiming the Positive

There are other steps you can take, such as challenging the messages of the past. You could say, "Who said they were right?" And "That's what I believed then, and I'm learning healthier beliefs now." And "I'm going to evaluate myself in a new way, the way God sees me in Jesus Christ."

If you read the following statements out loud morning and evening for the next month, your negative thoughts and feelings would have a difficult time staying in place, because now the truth has a foothold.

I Am Accepted ...

John 1:12	I am God's child.
John 15:15	I am Christ's friend.
Romans 5:1	I have been justified.
1 Corinthians 6:17	I am united with the Lord, and I am one spirit with him.
1 Corinthians 6:19-20	I have been bought with a price. I belong to God.
1 Corinthians 12:27	I am a member of Christ's body.
Ephesians 1:1	I am a saint.
Ephesians 1:5	I have been adopted as God's child.
Ephesians 2:18	I have direct access to God through the Holy Spirit.
Colossians 1:14	I have been redeemed and forgiven of all my sins.
Colossians 2:10	I am complete in Christ.

I Am Secure ...

Romans 8:1-2	I am free forever.
Romans 8:28	I am assured that all things work together for good.
Romans 8:31	I am free from any condemning charges against me.
Romans 8:35	I cannot be separated from the love of God.
2 Corinthians 1:21-22	I have been established, anointed, and sealed by God.
Colossians 3:3	I am hidden with Christ in God.
Philippians 1:6	I am confident that the good work that God has begun in me will be perfected.

2 Timothy 1:7	I have not been given a spirit of fear but of power, love, and a sound mind.
Hebrews 4:16	I can find grace and mercy in time of need.
1 John 5:18	I am born of God, and the evil one cannot touch me.

I Am Significant ...

Matthew 5:13-14	I am the salt and light of the earth.
John 15:1, 5	I am the branch of the true vine, a channel of his life.
John 15:16	I have been chosen and appointed to bear fruit.
Acts 1:8	I am a personal witness of Christ's.
1 Corinthians 3:16	I am God's temple.
2 Corinthians 5:18	I am a minister of reconciliation for God.
2 Corinthians 6:1	I am God's co-worker (1 Cor 3:9).
Ephesians 2:6	I am sealed with Christ in the heavenly realm.
Ephesians 2:18	I am God's workmanship.
Ephesians 3:12	I may approach God with freedom and confidence.
Philippians 4:13	I can do all things through Christ who strengthens me.[7]

So what will you do with your black thoughts now? They're uninvited guests, and you don't want them barging in. They don't own you or control you. You have to give them control for them to stay in your house. Evict them. If you think, *I'm helpless; I never do anything right; I can't get organized; I'll never figure this out;* or *Something must be wrong with me,* where's the evidence? Analyze each black thought. Challenge it. If you want to compare, compare your black thoughts with thoughts that are just the opposite. You'll like the difference. Whenever you're sad or blue or discouraged, ask yourself the comparative question: *What would I be thinking if I were basing this on a positive truth?* Then write it down. That's what to concentrate on. It's just as possible as focusing on the black thoughts.

Chapter 8

Beware of Relationships That Lead to Discouragement and the Blues

Relationships are one of the most significant elements of life. They are all around us. Commercials and TV programs are built on them. We think about them, talk about them, and experience them.

We were created to be in relationships, and most of our lives are spent in various relationships. Take them away, and our existence becomes sterile. They have the potential for happiness and fulfillment but also for discouragement and depression. This is why it's important to talk about them in this book. We need to consider healthy and unhealthy relationships.

Where do people experience the most painful rejections? Usually in dating or marriage. Where is it really easy to become discouraged? Usually in dating or marriage. Much of the material in this chapter deals with issues especially pertinent to people who are dating, making decisions about who they might like to marry and make a home with. But underlying principles apply to any friendship. What kind of relationships foster depression?

What Is Relationship Depression?

There's one factor to be considered when examining a relationship, no matter at what level the relationship exists. A relationship is going to be either a *depleting* or a *replenishing* one. A depleting relationship is one in which you are with someone who drains you emotionally and spiritually. It taps into your energy reserves in some way. It can happen in a long-term dating relationship or in a marriage. Being around this type of person is just plain hard work. At first the relationship may seem workable, but soon it becomes an exercise in depletion and coping. And the result can be discouragement or depression.

Relationship depression is the phrase used to describe the results of a depleting relationship. It's used to describe the sad or angry feelings caused by relational conflict and disappointments; it also refers to the absence of a meaningful relationship. Sometimes relationship depression occurs because of our own low self-esteem, poor choices, or lack of interpersonal skills or because of carefully hidden deficits in those we've chosen.

This depression can occur in a romantic relationship or a friendship and whether we're married or single. Many married individuals have experienced severe disappointment over what they thought marriage would be like. I've talked to many who claim their spouses turned into different people within weeks of their marriage. The person who during the courtship was attentive, considerate, a good listener, and communicative became just the opposite. Unfortunately, many spouses end up being victims of courtship deception.

When conflict and hassle become the norm rather than harmony and fulfillment, disappointment and even anger can be expected.

Sometimes relationship depression occurs because of childhood experiences with parents, teachers, siblings, or friends. It could range from rejection to abuse but it all hurts. Whenever you have an emotional investment in another person and expect your emotional needs to be met by that person but they're not, there's a possibility of relationship depression.

Men and women experience this form of depression, but women are more prone to it, because they are more socially connected and more apt to define who they are through relationships. Many women allow the pain of others to become their own. Culturally, women more than men are encouraged to meet the needs of and please others. They're also encouraged to focus on relationship more than achievement. And women tend to assume way too much responsibility for maintaining a relationship, even to the extent of not learning to take care of themselves. What's more, if a relationship has problems, a woman views it as a personal failure. If there is a repetitive pattern of problems or failures, she comes to expect relational difficulties. That's a sure sign of pessimistic discouragement. (And these experiences feed negative thoughts.)

Some women face these tendencies and their roles in less-than-satisfying relationships. They acknowledge the problems, grieve over losses, learn from them, make a course correction, and go on with their lives. Others, unfortunately, deny the pain or suffer in silence. It's natural to try to avoid pain, especially in relationships. Look at all the books that are available on how to have a good relationship! I've seen numerous women (and men) who go from one relationship to another repeating the same patterns. They fail to learn from the previous experience and keep doing what they've always done to connect with another person.[1]

Varieties of Unhealthy Relationships

Let's look at some varieties of unhealthy relational experience. Do any seem familiar to you, in that it is feeding a blue mood?

An Out-of-Balance Relationship

Have you experienced an out-of-balance relationship? This is one where you care more for the other person than that person cares about you. Or vice versa. Either way, the relationship is out of balance. It's tilting. One pursues while the other wants to pull back. A constant diet of this is unhealthy.

Sometimes the one who is not as invested in the relationship consciously tries to become more interested, believing that camaraderie or love will develop over time. When it doesn't, discouragement or the blues can set in.

You may think that this contrast in how you respond to each other simply indicates differences in your personalities. Perhaps, but it may also be lack of interest or caring.

It's difficult to admit that you may care more for the other person than he or she does for you. When you think about it, you get a sinking feeling in the pit of your stomach. And then you may rationalize yourself out of accepting the facts, or you may move into a state of denial.

I've seen the shock on a husband's or wife's face in marriage counseling when that person discovers the spouse's commitment level to the marriage is totally different from what the husband or wife thought it to be. It is sad that some of these marriages had existed (there is no other word to describe it—just existing!) with such disparate commitments for decades.

What are some indications that a relationship is a mismatch—that you have a higher level of interest in the relationship than the one you care about?

- You initiate most of the contact in the relationship.
- If this is a romantic attachment, you initiate most of the affectionate advances, such as holding hands, hugging, kissing.
- You're the plan maker; the other just seems to go along.
- You sacrifice to do things for the other or make life more agreeable, but you don't see this reciprocated.
- You're excited about the relationship, while the other person just seems to be along for the ride.
- You talk about your relationship and possible future plans, but this strikes an unresponsive chord with your partner.

If this is the pattern, the initiator's positive attitude will erode in time, the other's nonresponsiveness being experienced as a form of rejection.

Could this be just differences in personalities? Possibly. But if so, you can expect the person to be this way for the long term. Is this disparity what you want? Whether it's a personality difference or the other person really doesn't care as much as you do, either way, you'll eventually get weary of being the initiator.

The Rescuing Relationship

When I was in high school and college, some of my friends had summer jobs as lifeguards on the beaches and public pools. To me, lifeguarding was a dream job. These guys were in the sun all day, usually surrounded by kids their own age.

The hours were good and the scenery was great! As summer came to an end, I'd say to them, "What a great summer job you had! I'll bet you're sorry it's over."

Many of them surprised me by saying, "Not really. I'm glad to be getting back to school. I'm tired of constantly rescuing people."

When it comes to relationships, some people never tire of being rescuers. They live for it. Yet there's a problem with that. A relationship is *not* going to work if either one of you habitually rescues the other.

In a healthy relationship, you want to be there for the other person, and the other person wants to be there for you. But a relationship isn't healthy if you're the one who is always there for your partner, and he's like a ghost when you need him.

Sometimes you may be the one who takes the initiative to rescue. Or your partner insists that you rescue him, either by solving his problem or protecting him from the consequences of his behavior.

When you rescue on a continual basis, you're teaching the other person that there's no need for him to change, because you'll bail him out. He won't learn from past blunders, either.

If you rescue others, what do you expect from them? Thanks, appreciation, perhaps even reciprocation. But in a close relationship, you'll often find this response nonexistent—especially if your partner is a taker. Why? When you rescue others, you're exerting some type of control over them. In time they may end up resenting you for it. The unspoken, subtle message conveyed to them is "I'm better than you are, and you're not capable of handling things yourself." They could get discouraged and so will you.[2]

I've seen rescuers repeat this pattern with different partners. They seem to be attracted to people who need them.

The "Reforming" Relationship

Another relationship that fuels relationship depression is one in which the other person is not what you want him or her to be, or what you had hoped for, yet you find yourself thinking, *But he has such great potential!* You set yourself up for disappointment. And you find yourself holding onto false hope for change.

Remember, you can't reshape and reconstruct another person to this degree. I've seen people in marriages like this. They end up frustrated, critical, and feeling betrayed and hopelessly trapped. They would beg, plead, shout, and threaten their spouses, but to no avail. Discouragement? It's a constant companion.

Why do people continue such relationships? Some people feel called to be reformers. They like to reshape others, or at least try to. In doing so they ease the pain of looking at some of the issues of their own lives. I've seen both men and women do this to avoid their own problems.

Controlling Relationships

Some controllers and perfectionists are always trying to "help others fulfill their potential." This makes for a relationship that has low potential—when one person is full of anger and controlling tendencies or is a practicing perfectionist. In a marriage the unpleasantness quotient is quite high.

Perhaps the person you are in a relationship with isn't a perfectionist but just a controller. You will probably feel the same pressure with this type of person as you would with a perfectionist.

Both men and women use control to protect themselves from imagined concerns. Their use of control is part of their survival system. They believe that "the best defense is an offense"—the offensive strategy of staying in control. They live in fear of the results and consequences of not being in control. They're afraid of rejection, abandonment, hurt, disappointment, and of losing control itself. They may also be addicted to the respect, power, or emotional rush they get from controlling others.

I've counseled numerous "controllers." Their controlling tendencies are an integral part of their personalities. Some have even said, "I know I control. But why not? I have a lot to offer, and I know what I'm talking about. Why waste time? I want to see things happen—fast and efficiently. And I can do that!" That's sad. It can destroy people as well as relationships.

You may be thinking, *I know a number of relationships and marriages where one of them is a perfectionist or a controller. They're still together. It's working for them!* But is it? "Staying together" is not the same as having a relationship in which both individuals have the freedom to grow, to be all that God wants them to be, and to be comfortable with each other. If perfectionists or controllers can learn to give up these false bases for security, then growth can occur. I've seen this take place. But the work needs to begin before marriage.

The Trophy Relationship

Putting someone on a pedestal and seeing him or her as a "great catch" also lowers the relationship potential. If the person you are interested in lost his or her job or fame or beauty or other boastable quality, would you still be interested? Or if *you* lost those factors, would your partner or friend still be interested in you?

Unfortunately, some people use relationships or even marriage to move up in the world. If you're in this type of relationship, there are numerous factors to keep in mind. You could be giving that other person more influence, power, or control over you than you should. Are you bragging about this individual to impress others and elevate your status in their eyes? Are you elevating this person so much because you consider yourself less worthy or valuable or important than he or she is? If so, you need to see your own value and strengths. A relationship is made up of two individuals, each contributing unique gifts and strengths. Each of you contributes to the other; if it's one-sided, it won't work.

The Angry Relationship
Another potential relationship problem is when one or both parties are habitually angry. I don't mean the occasional normal angry response we all experience. I mean when one's life reflects a continual pattern of irritation, which, by the way, is anger. Relationships will bring out this tendency. A relationship can even be a factory for the production of anger.

When anger crosses the line of intensity and appropriate expression and becomes abuse, this, too, is a violation—with lasting results that could be worse than discouragement or depression. Many people in angry relationships never give such expressions of anger a thought. If they do, it's to think that it happens to others, never to them.

Abuse is any behavior that is designed to control or subjugate another person through the use of fear, humiliation, and verbal or physical assaults. "Physical" refers to brutal physical

contact that is not accidental. It can include pushing, grab-
bing, shoving, slapping, kicking, biting, choking, punching,
hitting with an object, sexual assault, or attacking with a knife
or gun.

But there is emotional abuse, as well. Scare tactics, insults,
yelling (shouting), temper tantrums, name-calling, and con-
tinuous criticism fall into this classification, as do withholding
privileges or affection and constantly blaming.

Surprised? Some feel this is just the way people live. But
such a lifestyle, though common, is neither appropriate nor
healthy. As you read these definitions, you may discover that
you grew up in a home that was abusive. Or you may be in an
abusive relationship now. Are there any signs of such a pattern
in your own life or in that of the other person in your relationship?

Wrap-Up

Perhaps you have found yourself in this chapter. If so, could
your relationship be contributing to a blue mood? What steps
can you take to turn your relationship into a healthy one or
leave an unhealthy dating experience?

This is what I propose you want and look for in a relationship that will minimize discouragement and the blues.

- You want to feel safe and secure in your relationship.
  You want to be able to breathe a sigh of relief and say,
  "It's nice to relax with someone, let down the protec-
  tive armor, and be myself."
- You want to feel supported and give support.
- You want to know you're not facing the world alone.

You want to feel you depend on someone to stand with you in difficult times, even when that person doesn't necessarily agree with your stand.

- You want to be and be with a supportive person, not only during difficult times, but also during good times. When you support others, you encourage them, help them dream and grow, even to the point that they exceed your own level of growth or ability. You use your strengths, capabilities, and skills to lift the other person above yourself.

- We all have a built-in, God-given need for a sense of belonging that comes from being accepted. It's easy to get along with people who accept you, open their hearts to you, and include you in their lives.

- You need a relationship with someone who cares about you—as you also care for and nurture that person. When you nurture someone, you invite him or her to take a special place in your heart. You express your care through words as well as your deeds.

Look for and be this kind of person. It's the best antidote and prevention against discouragement or the blues caused by unhealthy relationships.[3]

For assistance in building better relationships, see *Boundaries in Dating* by Henry Cloud and John Townsend (Zondervan, 2000) and *Relationships That Work and Those That Don't* by H. Norman Wright (Regal, 1998).

Chapter 9

Real-Life Solutions: Stepping Out

If you find you are becoming depressed, what can you do about it? First of all, check for any physical reasons; you may want to see your medical doctor. If there seems to be no physical cause, ask yourself two key questions. You may want to ask your spouse or a good friend to help you think them through:

What am I doing that might be bringing on my depression? Check your behavior to determine that it is consistent with Scripture. Ask yourself if you are doing anything to reinforce the depression.

What am I thinking about, or in what way am I thinking that might be making me depressed?

Look for your depression "trigger." Some triggers are obvious; you're readily aware of what prompted the depression. Other causes are more difficult to discover. You may want to keep the following questions on a card; when you're depressed refer to them to help you recall the thought or event that triggered the depression.

1. What did I do?
2. Where did I go?
3. With whom did I speak?
4. What did I see?
5. What did I read?
6. What was I thinking about?[1]

Changing Negative to Positive

Evaluate your thoughts and value judgments. We've already talked about negative thinking and "black thoughts." Remember, your thinking pattern *can* be changed. Consider and dwell on these Scriptures:

> For God did not give us a spirit of timidity, of cowardice, of craven and cringing and fawning fear, but [he has given us a spirit] of power and of love and of calm and well-balanced mind and discipline and self-control.
>
> 2 TIMOTHY 1:7, AMPLIFIED

> Be constantly renewed in the spirit of your mind— having a fresh mental and spiritual attitude.
>
> EPHESIANS 4:23, AMPLIFIED

> So brace up your minds; be sober—circumspect [morally alert]; set your hope wholly and unchangeably on the grace (divine favor) that is coming to you when Jesus Christ, the Messiah, is revealed.
>
> 1 PETER 1:13, AMPLIFIED

Scripture calls us to change our thinking patterns, our thoughts. But the Scriptures also state that the Holy Spirit is actively at work in influencing our minds and helping us to control our thoughts.

Here are two suggestions that have helped many people change from negative patterns to positive patterns. A physician asked a patient to keep a stopwatch with him and to start it when he had a negative thought and to stop it when a positive thought came in to replace it. He noted the blocks of time on a sheet of graph paper, and carried the watch and the paper with him wherever he went. Before this experiment, he felt that the negative thoughts were in his mind constantly. By timing them and putting them on a graph, he found that they did not occur as often as he had thought. The whole process of timing the thoughts helped him to develop methods of controlling the negative thoughts he did have. He began to take control of his life.

Another method of breaking a negative thinking pattern involves writing Philippians 4:6 on a three-by-five card: "Do not fret or have any anxiety about anything, but in every circumstance and in everything by prayer and petition [definite requests] with thanksgiving continue to make your wants known to God" (AMPLIFIED). On the other side of the card write the word *stop*. Whenever you struggle with negative thinking, take out the card, hold it with the word *stop* facing you, and say the word out loud. Turn the card over and read the verse out loud. (If you are at work or with other people, you may read silently.) Do this regularly, and you will defeat the negative thought pattern and replace it with the positive thoughts of the Scriptures.

The next step in overcoming depression is to ask yourself several questions in these following areas:

Awareness. Am I depressed? To what degree? Why? Has this happened before?

Motivation. What am I gaining from being depressed? Am I being excused from certain responsibilities? Have I undergone any major changes or stresses during the past few months or years? How am I trying to adjust to them?

Decision. Am I going to continue to be depressed?

Action. What kind of environment am I in? Is it helping me to come out of my depression? What actions can I take to reduce or eliminate my depression?

Action can be broken down into a number of areas.

Examine Habits

Look at your eating and sleeping habits to see if these ought to be changed. If your appetite is poor and you are losing weight, try very hard to eat frequent small amounts of food.

Stay Active

Are you following your normal life routine, or are you withdrawing by staying in bed longer, staying away from friends, letting the dishes stack up in the sink, or avoiding regular activities? Are you cutting yourself off from your friends and family? If so, it is important to force yourself to stay active. Remember that a depressed person begins behaving and acting in such a way that the depression is reinforced. You must break the depressive pattern of behavior by yourself or by asking someone to help you.

Try to get out of the house, even for very short periods of time. You might go out for the paper in the morning after breakfast; go walk around the block or to a favorite place or store.

Initiate some kind of physical activity that you ordinarily like or think you might like. It is difficult to remain depressed when you are singing, swimming, riding a bicycle, jogging, playing tennis, and so on.

Exercise is an active approach to life. Depression, on the other hand, is a malady that creates passivity; inactivity gradually becomes the style of life. Exercise is not only partial inoculation against depression, but it can also be part of the treatment. Active people or those who engage in regular exercise each week report a better sense of psychological well-being than those who do not exercise.

Dr. Otto Appenzeller of the University of New Mexico has found that the nervous system releases hormones called catecholamines during marathon running. He discovered that the catecholamines in marathon runners were increased to 600 percent above normal. It is also known that these hormones are low in people suffering from depression. So it would appear that the connection between running and the release of these hormones could be generalized to include moderate forms of exercise.[2]

In another experimental study, a number of depressed clients became involved in a gradual planned program of running. They reported reduced tension and improved sleep, and depressive symptoms began to lift.[3]

In addition to hormonal changes, are there other reasons that can account for the lifting of depression through exercise? Yes. Participating in a pleasant activity can improve one's outlook. A sense of success and mastery can develop as one continues an exercise program. Self-discipline, patience, and endurance can reinforce a person's self-image. And the active nature of exercise counteracts the passivity and helplessness of depression.

Before engaging in any type of exercise program, get a physical checkup. Find a program you can learn to enjoy, and move into it gradually.

I did not really have a regular exercise program until 1980, when I experienced a stress reaction or burnout. During that time I was also depressed. My physician told me that there wasn't much wrong with me except that I was like a one-ton truck trying to do the work of a two-ton truck. I didn't need a major overhaul but a minor tune-up. He also had the audacity to tell me that the only other thing that was wrong with me was that I was carrying twelve extra pounds! His words were the extra push I needed to get into action.

Gradually I lost eighteen pounds, began to ride an indoor bicycle, and with the encouragement of two friends learned to play racquetball. For years I've ridden an indoor bicycle each morning, and for seventeen years I played racquetball two to three mornings a week. I discovered more energy, endurance, alertness, and quickness than I had ten, fifteen, or even twenty-five years ago. Exercise does make a difference in your physical, emotional, and spiritual well-being.

Communicate

Let your spouse know that you are depressed. Ask him or her to listen to you as you explain it. If you want a response, ask for one; if not, ask him or her only to listen supportively. If you are angry with your spouse or someone else, discuss your feelings with that person and get them out into the open.

In all depressions, you need a person you can trust (a family member or friend) to whom you can complain and express feelings of anger. If you don't have one, find one—and let your feelings out!

If you can push yourself to do it, try to see family members and friends as much as possible, but for very short periods of time. Don't try to entertain in your home, but visit other people informally and briefly.

If it is difficult to talk to the people you live with, write a note. Explain briefly, for example, that it is of no use to you if they try to lift your spirits by kidding you, however well-intended they may be, if that kidding is only aggravating your negative mood.

If your friends and family are the kind of people who think you will be strengthened by being scolded and criticized, tell them they are mistaken. You need encouragement, support, and firmness.

Keep Your Schedule

Each day, either by yourself or with another person's help, make a list of what you would do during the day if you were not depressed. After you have made this list in detail, work out a plan to follow that list each day.

Try to keep your daily routine. If you work outside the home, try to go to work each day. It is more beneficial for you to get up in the morning, get dressed, have breakfast, go to your place of work, and go through the motions of working than to remain home in bed with your discomforting thoughts.

If your work is in the home, follow the same procedure. Consider your daily chores important. You may feel, *it doesn't matter what I do.* But it does.

Another way of developing a pattern of positive behavior is to make an extensive list (with help if necessary) of pleasant events. After the list is made, select several events to do each day. A pleasant events schedule is not a panacea for all depression, but often you can break the pattern of depression through your behavior. Most people feel better when they engage in pleasant activities.

As you schedule activities, try listing and fixing in your mind exactly what you expect to enjoy when you engage in that activity. For example:

ACTIVITY PLANNED _____

DATE PLANNED FOR _____

I WILL ENJOY _____

_____

I WILL ENJOY _____

_____

I WILL ENJOY _____

_____

Seek Positive Input

Read some of the books suggested in this book. These resources will assist you in developing a thinking pattern that could lift your depression. Focus upon appropriate Scriptures. Each morning read these passages; put them on posters and place them around the house: Psalm 27:1-3; 37:1-7; Isaiah 26:3; 40:28-31. Don't cut yourself off from others. Continue to attend worship. Seek fellowship with others who care for you and are supportive.

Prayer and Depression

Is it possible to pray one's way out of depression? Many individuals have tried to do so but found no change. It depends upon the type or cause of depression. If sin is the direct cause of depression, then prayer that includes confession, repentance, and the acceptance of forgiveness can rid you of the depression. But all too often a depressed individual thinks his depression is caused by sin when in reality it is not. This is often a reflection of the person's feeling of worthlessness that accompanies depression.

Genuine praise for who God is and the strength that he gives us can be an aid in handling our depression. But in a depressed state we probably do not feel full of praise, so turning to this positive thought takes some effort. Taking the time and energy to list our blessings and then specifically mention them to God in prayer may give us a more positive perspective. The best way to do this is with another person who is not depressed and knows your life quite well.

Assessing Activity

As I said earlier in the chapter, one of the best remedies for depression is to become more active. Changing one's level of activity has several benefits, but it is often difficult. It means going counter to what you are feeling. You will need to challenge the thoughts and ideas that keep you from being active.

Increasing your activity is a definite way of changing your thinking. When you are inactive, you are likely to think of yourself as inadequate, lazy, and worthless. A good reason to become more active is to challenge those ideas; by being more active you create evidence that you are not like that. You show yourself that you can get started and accomplish something.

Studies indicate that activity will improve your mood. Usually the more you do, the better you feel. Activity also provides a helpful diversion from your depression by distracting your mind from unpleasant thoughts.

Activity will also counteract the fatigue that you find with depression. Paradoxically, when you are depressed, you need to do more to gain more energy. When you are not depressed, you are revived by rest and inactivity. Studies also show that activity will increase motivation. By completing a simple task successfully, you will be motivated to try some other task.

With depression, you must do what you don't feel like doing before you feel like doing it! This is strange, but true. And this phenomenon is not limited to a depressed state, for many people find that by doing a behavior first, their feelings come in line with that behavior.

By being physically active, you can stimulate your mental ability. Solutions to previously unsolvable situations can be discovered in a mode of activity.

When you become active, you find that other people positively reinforce what you are doing. You no longer have to hear them suggest that you "do something."

Activity Record

The following is an activity record that you might use as a model to help you keep track of your activities if you are depressed. This written exercise is important, because when you are depressed, your memory is selective. It forgets the positive while remembering only the negative.

Weekly Activity Record[4]

Time	Mon	Tues	Wed	Thurs	Fri	Sat	Sun
AM/PM	Activity	Activity	Activity	Activity	Activity	Activity	Activity
6-7							
7-8							
8-9							
9-10							
10-11							
11-12							
12-1							
1-2							
2-3							
3-4							
4-5							
5-6							
6-7							
7-8							
8-9							
9-10							
10-11							
11-12							

Record hour by hour what you do for a week. Next to the actual activity indicate how much satisfaction you felt on a scale from 0 to 5 (0 meaning none and 5 meaning great). This tabulation can help you see what it is that gives you pleasure and satisfaction.

Be aware of what you write. You may tend to write down a

negative such as "I did nothing." Yet perhaps your doing nothing involved watching a TV program and drinking a cup of tea. Record that activity instead, because doing something is not nothing. If you are unsure, you could ask someone to help you identify all that you are doing that you could be overlooking.

Keep this record for several weeks to help you identify what does and does not give you satisfaction and to see what might be contributing to depression.

Graph Over Time
Sometimes you can keep a running hour-by-hour account of your activities to help you assess patterns and improvements. A day-by-day graph such as the following will show the amount of improvement you have made.

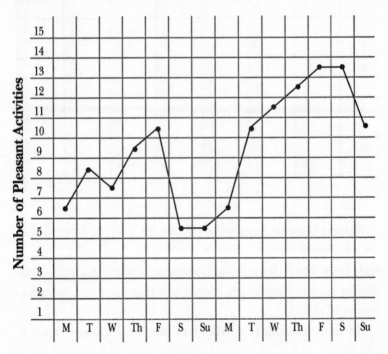

Planning a Schedule

It is also important for you to plan an actual schedule of what you will do. By scheduling your activities you are taking control of your life. It will also help you overcome indecisiveness, which is a common characteristic of depression. Keeping a schedule and scheduling activities will give you an opportunity to identify and counter self-defeating thoughts that keep you immobilized. By reviewing what you have already done and by looking over what you plan to do the next day, you will generate a different set of feelings about yourself.

Scheduling activity directly confronts a depressed person's tendency toward passivity. It may be helpful for you to pinpoint your passive thoughts and counter them with statements of activity. Here is an example of a woman who was interested in going back to college to take some classes. Listed below are her passive thoughts and her answers to the thoughts.

Ways to Keep Yourself Passive and Answers to Them[5]

Thoughts	*Answers*
It's too hard to find out about taking classes.	It's as difficult as it is— no more, no less. I've done many more difficult things.
I won't know what schools to call or what questions to ask.	The idea is to do it—not do it perfectly. It's better to do a poor job, to try to find out, than not to try at all.

I don't want to do it. I hate making phone calls.	That's what I think now—but earlier I wanted to do it. So whether or not I want to do it now is irrelevant. I'd better do it now, for my own good.
I don't think I'm up to doing it. I'll wait until I feel more like doing it.	I don't know for sure. I'm not a mind reader. I'll experiment and see what I can do. Inspiration comes from activity, not the other way around.
I've wasted so much time already. When I start to do it, it reminds me of wasted time.	I didn't waste time. I just did something different with that time. Now the question is, what do I want to do with this time—more of the same or something different?
I can't decide which school to call first.	Call the one that comes first in alphabetical order. Calling the least helpful is better than not calling one at all.

How do you plan an activity schedule? Very simply. Be flexible; don't set up a rigid pattern that you cannot change. Stick with the general plan. If you miss an activity, just let it go and schedule it another time. If you finish a task early, don't start the next task until the set time. Do something enjoyable until that time. Treat yourself! Schedule activities in half-hour and one-hour intervals. Don't plan activities that are too specific or too general. Don't bite off more than you can chew. Enjoying the activity at a satisfying pace is part of the plan.

Let's say you need to get a handle on the task of house-keeping. If you have "let the house go" for several weeks, it may take several days or weeks to establish some order. That extended time is all right! Break your large tasks into smaller tasks. Grade them from easy to difficult. List the various jobs that need to be done, whether your task is to clean the basement, the yard, or the living room. List what you will do within that overall job. Cleaning the living room may involve picking up all the magazines, dusting, vacuuming, washing the two windows, getting the dog hair off the easy chair, and so forth.

Don't be surprised if you are tempted to skip scheduling your activities. Here are some typical sabotage techniques you may try to use on yourself and some ways to counter them.

Statement: "I don't know if I can think of any activities to schedule."

Answer: You are probably having trouble thinking of some. Why not list activities that you must do each day (such as eating and dressing), activities that give you pleasure, and activities that bring a sense of accomplishment?

Statement: "I have never kept records and I have never been able to work under a schedule."

Answer: Scheduling is a simple skill that can be learned. If it is difficult to keep an hour-by-hour schedule, you could list one task from eight o'clock until ten o'clock, another from ten until twelve, and one from one until six. This is a good way to begin.

Statement: "I have so much difficulty with distractions. I just do not follow through."

Answer: Make a list of typical distractions. Identify what they are. Then formulate in writing how you will refuse to give in to each distraction. You may need to unplug the TV, phone, and computer and reconnect them when the task is completed. It is also all right to tell the caller that you are busy but will call back at a later time. Write yourself a contract such as "I will complete thirty minutes of housecleaning and then read *Guideposts* for twenty minutes."

Use signs around the house to remind you of your commitments and schedule. Make them creatively unusual to attract your attention. When you start a task, select the easiest and simplest so that you are almost guaranteed success.

Seek Help

You may want to reread these chapters and select what might help you the most.

Sometimes the solution for your depression is going for help. And sometimes it is difficult to admit we have a problem to the extent we need to ask someone for help. But consider some of these indicators that help is needed. You need the assistance of someone else when:

Your depression has lasted longer than six months.

Your depression is hurting your family or your work performance.

You have recurring episodes of depression.

You have suicidal thoughts.

You are having delusional thoughts.

You are having difficulty sleeping or are having physical discomfort to the extent that it is affecting your health.

Where do you go for help? You may want to talk to your minister *if* he is knowledgeable about depression. If you have not had a complete and thorough physical in the last year, talk to your physician. But again, it is important to ask questions and discover if your doctor believes in both counseling and medication. Some depression can be treated best by medication, but other conditions respond best to counseling. And some need both.

A Christian psychologist, psychiatrist, marriage counselor, or qualified lay counselor can be helpful. Ask your church, friends, or minister for a referral to a qualified professional. These individuals can be the instrument that God uses not only to give you the assistance you need for your depression but to assist you in your spiritual growth as well.

Remember that it *is* possible to overcome discouragement, rejection, and the blues. You're not dealing with them alone. Invite Jesus into the process of changing your life. He understands. He guides us. And he gives us the power we need.

Remember Paul's words to young Timothy. Claim them as yours:

For God did not give us a spirit of timidity—of cowardice, of craven and cringing and fawning fear—but [he has given us a spirit] of power and of love and of calm and well-balanced mind and discipline and self-control.

2 TIMOTHY 1:7, AMPLIFIED

Notes

ONE
Fighting Discouragement: Going for Broke

1. Adapted from Kathleen Fischer and Thomas Hart, *Facing Discouragement* (Mahwah, N.J.: Paulist, 1997), 4–9.
2. Fischer and Hart, 16–17.
3. Charles Swindoll, *Strengthening Your Grip* (Nashville, Tennessee: Word, 1982).
4. Adapted from Paul L. Walker, *Courage for Crisis Living* (Grand Rapids, Mich.: Fleming H. Revell, 1978), 75.
5. Walker, 94–95.
6. Adapted from David Viscott, *Risking* (New York: Pocket 1977), 18–21, 28.
7. Adapted from H. Norman Wright, *Your Tomorrows Can Be Different* (Grand Rapids, Mich.: Fleming H. Revell, 1992), 110–12.
8. Adapted from H. Norman Wright, *Making Peace With Your Past* (Grand Rapids, Mich.: Fleming H. Revell, Spire, 1985), 39–40.
9. Bob George, *Growing Free in Grace* (Eugene, Ore.: Harvest House, 1991), 128.
10. Adapted from Wright, *Your Tomorrows Can Be Different,* 132.
11. Walker, 29.

TWO
Rejection—It Hurts

1. Lewis Carroll, *Alice's Adventures in Wonderland and Through the Looking-Glass* (New York: New American Library, 1960), 66.
2. Elizabeth Skoglund, *Growing Through Rejection* (Wheaton, Ill.: Tyndale, 1983), 41–42.
3. Skoglund, 93.
4. Lloyd John Ogilvie, *Facing the Future Without Fear* (Ann Arbor, Mich.: Servant, 1999), 94–95.
5. Skoglund, 58.
6. Adapted from William J. Knaus, *Do It Now* (Englewood Cliffs, N.J.: Prentice Hall, 1979), 64–71.

THREE
Overcoming Rejection

1. J.I. Packer, *Knowing God* (Downers Grove, Ill.: InterVarsity Press, 1973), 37.
2. Joseph Cooke, *Free for the Taking* (Grand Rapids, Mich.: Fleming H. Revell, 1975), 29.
3. Adapted from Elayne Savage, *Don't Take It Personally* (Oakland, Calif.: New Harbinger, 1997), 41–42.
4. Adapted from Savage, 4–5.
5. David Burns, *Feeling Good* (New York: Signet, 1980), 258.
6. Frank Houghton, *Amy Carmichael of Dohnavur* (Fort Washington, Pa.: Christian Literature Crusade, 1979), cited in Ogilvie, 104.
7. Ogilvie, 93.

FOUR
Depression—What's It All About?

1. Adapted from Siang-Yang Tan and John Ortberg Jr., *Coping With Depression* (Grand Rapids, Mich.: Baker, 1995), 14–15.

2. Adapted from Ellen McGrath, *Women and Depression: Risk Factor and Treatment Issues* (Washington, D.C.: American Psychological Association, 1990), 22.

3. Adapted from Tan and Ortberg, 21.

4. Adapted from Ellen McGrath, *When Feeling Bad Is Good* (New York: Henry Holt, 1992), 23–29.

5. Julia Thorne with Larry Rothstein, *You Are Not Alone* (New York: HarperCollins, 1992), 129.

6. Adapted from Brenda Poinsett, *Why Do I Feel This Way?* (Colorado Springs: NavPress, 1996), 36–37.

7. Richard Foster, *Celebration of Discipline* (San Francisco: Harper & Row, 1978), 89–91.

8. F.F. Flach, *The Secret Strength of Depression* (Philadelphia: Lippincott, 1974), 41–42.

9. Adapted from McGrath, *When Feeling Bad Is Good*, 34-39.

10. Adapted from McGrath, *Women and Depression*, 4.

11. Adapted from Demitri F. Papolos and Janice Papolos, *Overcoming Depression* (New York: Harper & Row, 1988), 47.

12. See M. Goed, *The Good News About Depression* (New York: Bantam, 1986), 195–203.

13. Adapted from McGrath, *When Feeling Bad Is Good*, 40–46.

FIVE

Myths About Depression

1. Adapted from Tan and Ortberg, 27.
2. Adapted from Mitch Golant and Susan K. Golant, *What to Do When Someone You Love Is Depressed* (New York: Henry Holt, 1996), 12-13, 120-21.
3. Poinsett, 89.
4. Adapted from *Depression Is a Treatable Illness* (Rockville, Md.: U.S. Department of Health and Human Services, April 1993), 4.
5. Adapted from Poinsett, 89–91.

SIX

The Blue Mood

1. Adapted from Robert Hirschfeld, M.D., with Susan Meltsner, *When the Blues Won't Go Away* (New York: Macmillan, 1991), 12–20.
2. Adapted from John Bradshaw, *Bradshaw On: The Family* (Hollywood, Fla.: Health Communications, 1988), 3.
3. Bradshaw, 4–5.
4. Adapted from Bradshaw, 1–2.
5. Adapted from Hirschfeld, 29–43.
6. Hirschfeld, 28.

SEVEN
Triggers That Set Off the Blues

1. Charles Swindoll, *Come Before Winter* (Portland, Ore.: Multnomah, 1985), 239.
2. Robert Hirschfeld, adapted from David Burns, *Feeling Good* (New York: Signet, 1980), 56.
3. Adapted from Julian L. Simon, *Good Mood* (Chicago: Open Court, 1993), 87.
4. Adapted from Simon, 44–45.
5. Adapted from Simon, 97–98, 126.
6. Adapted from Simon, 47–48, 126–28.
7. From Neil Anderson, *Freedom in Christ Ministries.*

EIGHT
Beware of Relationships
That Lead to Discouragement and the Blues

1. Adapted from Ellen McGrath, *When Feeling Bad Is Good,* 116–30.
2. Adapted from Carolyn Bushong, *Seven Dumbest Relationship Mistakes Smart People Make* (New York: Villard, 1997), 152–72.
3. Adapted from H. Norman Wright, *Relationships That Work and Those That Don't* (Ventura, Calif.: Regal, 1998), 115–28.

NINE

Real-Life Solutions: Stepping Out

1. Adapted from Archibald Hart, *Coping With Depression in the Ministry and Other Helping Professions* (Waco, Tex.: Word, 1987), 68.
2. Adapted from Richard R. Berg and Christine McCartney, *Depression and the Integrated Life* (New York: Alta House, 1981), 117.
3. See John H. Greist, Marjorie H. Klein, Roger R. Eishens, John Faris, Alan S. Gurman, and William P. Morgan, "Running as Treatment for Depression," *Comprehensive Psychiatry,* 20 (1979), 44–54.
4. Adapted from Gary Emery, *A New Beginning* (New York: Simon & Schuster, 1981), 75.
5. Emery, 79.